T0066519

the SOUL
ILLUMINATED

First published by O-Books, 2010
O Books is an imprint of John Hunt Publishing Ltd., The Bothy, Deershot Lodge, Park Lane, Ropley,
Hants, SO24 0BE, UK
office1@o-books.net
www.o-books.net

Distribution in:	South Africa
	Stephan Phillips (pty) Ltd
UK and Europe	Email: orders@stephanphillips.com
Orca Book Services Ltd	Tel: 27 21 4489839 Telefax: 27 21 4479879
Home trade orders	
tradeorders@orcabookservices.co.uk	Text copyright Judith Pemell 2009
Tel: 01235 465521	
Fax: 01235 465555	ISBN: 978 1 84694 297 6
Export orders	
exportorders@orcabookservices.co.uk	
Tel: 01235 465516 or 01235 465517	
Fax: 01235 465555	
USA and Canada	Design: Tom Davies
NBN	
custserv@nbnbooks.com	All rights reserved. Except for brief quotations
Tel: 1 800 462 6420 Fax: 1 800 338 4550	in critical articles or reviews, no part of this
	book may be reproduced in any manner without
Australia and New Zealand	prior written permission from the publishers.
Brumby Books	
sales@brumbybooks.com.au	The rights of Judith Pemell as author have been
Tel: 61 3 9761 5535 Fax: 61 3 9761 7095	asserted in accordance with the Copyright,
	Designs and Patents Act 1988.
Far East (offices in Singapore, Thailand,	
Hong Kong, Taiwan)	A CIP catalogue record for this book is available
Pansing Distribution Pte Ltd	from the British Library.
kemal@pansing.com	
Tel: 65 6319 9939 Fax: 65 6462 5761	Printed by Digital Book Print

O Books operates a distinctive and ethical publishing philosophy in
all areas of its business, from its global network of authors to
production and worldwide distribution.

the SOUL ILLUMINATED

JUDITH PEMELL

BOOKS

Winchester, UK
Washington, USA

contents

part two
COMMUNION

For my spiritual family,
whose love and challenges
nurture enduring
spiritual growth.

*It is not necessary to get into all sorts of things
inside your head. On the contrary, a level head
and an honest heart are all that is needed.*

*No longer ruled by roller-coaster emotions,
your true nature of divinity
will ultimately begin to assert itself.
It will begin to exert its own influence.*

And you, the real you, will be freed.

Dadi Janki, *Wings of Soul*

introduction

It was a beautiful balmy winter in California in early 1984, when a series of events occurred which would quietly alter the course of my life. A feeling of excitement and anticipation had crept into my being during the very early days of the year. A new feeling, a kind of inner springtime seemed to be stirring as though I was opening up to something completely unknown and new. 'There is a tide in the affairs of men, which, taken at the flood leads on to fortune'. Shakespeare's words described perfectly how it was for me in 1984. The tide would inevitably leave no stone in my life unturned. I look back knowing my moment had come, and as much as I attempted to resist parts of what was happening, the flood would not, could not, be held back. It seemed as though an inner alarm had suddenly burst into life, signalling a time of movement, wresting me to the wilder shores of the unknown.

As an atheist I had no idea about spirituality. My early religious education had failed to enthral me or address any of my burning questions about the meaning of life. Foremost among these was 'who am I?' Perhaps one of the greatest curiosities of human existence is that 'I' don't know who 'I' am, or how this 'I' feels.

In *Life After Life*,[2] Raymond A. Moody writes that people who have had a near-death experience commonly report the feeling of 'utter peace, quietness, extreme comfort and relaxation', the instant they experience leaving their physical body. They describe with acute awareness, all that was happening to the body, and the 'death' scene taking place, but they felt no emotion or physical connection to it. In addition, many of these people report having no subsequent fear of death, and some express anger and resentment at being 'brought back'. For most, there is the realisation that their understanding of themselves has profoundly expanded and that there is much more to learn about

1

life. The way these people describe their experiences of 'death' using terms such as peace, comfort, stillness, detachment and awareness, is precisely the way a yogi might describe her or his meditation experience.

Watching a cat stretch out in the sun on a winter's day, purring softly, I see an image of relaxation, contentment, ease, peace and stillness. I would come to learn that the soul experience is something like this. Coming to understand the soul is perhaps one of the simplest yet most curious of journeys, and it is reassuring to know we do not have to die to have this experience.

What is the value, if any, of understanding the soul? For some people it may be of passing interest, yet for those of us who experience a deep mystical yearning for this enlightened state, it is the Holy Grail, the key to the tantalising mystery of existence. Siddhartha's search for the 'source of the self within the self' leads him on a spiritual quest, eloquently envisioned by author Herman Hesse in *Siddhartha*, through ascetic withdrawal into sensual immersion, and finally to the banks of the great river, a landscape that reflects his crossing from the world of flesh into the transcendent realisation of spirit.

Through my own journey, it has taken many years for me to come to a deep comprehension of the subtle self. Experiencing and penetrating the 'I' in yoga has gradually transformed my old state of consciousness into one which rests on spiritual truth, and with it has come a freedom I could never have imagined. Truth, it is said, makes the soul dance in ecstasy. It is this truth that unlocks the soul's potential and freedom to 'be'. This *potential* relates to that in us which is great, noble and complete, but is usually hidden. It is the ability to open our hearts in an unlimited way, to rise above any circumstance and imbue our lives and activities with truth, love, creativity and higher purpose.

The spiritual journey releases the intrinsic beauty, meaning and extraordinary capacity each of us has to be simply, humbly and magnanimously human. This is the value of knowing the subtle self; it means becoming fully and wonderfully human. The *soul illuminated* is like a flawless diamond, whose radiance gleams brightly through the darkness, lighting the way.

Many of the perceptions I express here have been informed by my learning and practice of Raja Yoga Meditation, as taught by the Brahma Kumaris World Spiritual University, but significantly by my own intimate spiritual journey over the past twenty years. The experiences and people I write about are a distillation of many influences and experiences in my life, work and relationships.

part one

the SUBTLE SELF

*In touch with its own eternity
the soul abides and
is drawn irresistibly to God,
the eternal companion.*

chapter one

SOMETHING'S
HAPPENING

When I was four or five, my mother, enthralled by a book she was reading, would burst into praise about the details of it across the dinner table. The book was partly about a young boy whose story was very unusual. He lived in a magical, far-away land called Tibet. My mother explained how, out of all the little boys in Tibet, he was identified at the age of two as a reincarnation of the Dalai Lama. She described how the people who were searching for him put him through a series of unusual tests. He was shown a variety of objects, some of which were from his past 'Incarnation' as the Dalai Lama, and he was able to enthusiastically and clearly recognise the relevant objects immediately. As a young boy growing up, he would fast and sit in meditation for days at a time! The book was called *Seven Years in Tibet*.[4] I cannot remember whether my mother attempted to explain reincarnation to me then, but I knew what she meant anyway, because at that age I was having frequent flashbacks of my own last life. As a tiny four-year-old girl, I would suddenly experience myself to be a very tall man, standing head and shoulders above everyone. The amusement this image brought to me was part of my inner life as a child and was never articulated or shared then. Like my mother, I was fascinated with the young Dalai Lama and by the age of four, the seed of mystical enquiry had been sown in me.

Another story which fascinated me later in life was Shirley MacLaine's compelling *Out on a Limb*.[5] It begins with a series of experiences of synchronicity, strangely coincidental events that hooked her curiosity and began guiding her steps in an unknown direction. Her story slowly unfolds like an adventure mystery as she begins to unravel a new understanding of herself, culminating in a spontaneous and powerful experience in the Andes mountains. The great significance of her out-of-body experience in Peru, which she describes succinctly, is that she clearly realises herself as an aware, conscious living being, quite separate from her physical body. Her journey is about the connection between mind, body and spirit, and how the learning she gains enables her to live her life 'as an almost transformed human being'.[6]

Synchronicity seems to play a role in engaging our mystical curiosity and setting off the alarm that begins to awaken us. Spiritual awakening does not occur through a rational, deductive mental process. It tends to arrive unexpectedly and is not something that can be induced, rationalised, manipulated or faked. The absolute innocence of spiritual awakening is what characterises it. Synchronistic events are the unmistakable clues that 'hook us in' through curiosity and lead us into the unknown, following their thread if we are willing to be led.

During the early 1990s, I submitted an abstract for a conference paper on addictions. My paper specifically addressed the spiritual dimensions of addiction and the recovery process, and at its core was information about the soul and a statistical study on the effects of meditation on people in recovery from addictions. When the abstract was accepted I began to feel slightly uncomfortable with my own daring, for the theme of the conference was strongly scientific. As the occasion drew near, my feeling of discomfort turned into anxiety. I was reconciled to the fact that I would probably be ridiculed by my colleagues, then I rationalised that no one would attend the session, since there were five much more interesting sessions running parallel. The day of the presentation arrived and, feeling just a little unnerved, I took a seat in the auditorium, early.

The hall filled quickly, I had grossly underestimated the intentions of my colleagues. Towards the rear I could see a couple of my fellow meditators and a friend who had come to lend moral support. As I rose to give the paper I noticed people were standing at the back. The gathering was very silent as I launched into my presentation, waiting for them to become bored and inattentive. However, they listened attentively and responded with genuine interest, curiosity and warmth during question time. At the end of the day, a gathering of those who had attended the session formed quite randomly in one of the bars. People sat sprawled in chairs, with many on the floor in a loose and untidy circle. A spontaneous discussion of the paper opened up and, as people began sharing, an unusual sense of intimacy and connection quickly enveloped us. A colleague from Melbourne said that when the presentation got going he had an overwhelming sense of 'something happening'. As the sharing in the bar became more intimate he kept singing softly, 'something's happening!' Something was definitely happening. A mystical rapport was becoming palpable within the group, touching each one of us in a warm and heartfelt way. I felt humbled and deeply moved. For me, this was a lesson in faith and trust. The experience of that day etched itself in my heart.

ະ⊱◈⊰ະ

By the time I met Brian in Los Angeles a number of 'incidents' had occurred, especially three separate events of the kind that turn up in horror movies. The first of these happened at about three o'clock in the morning.

While I was asleep I became aware of a male voice speaking to me inside my head saying, 'Judi, wake up!' As I was in a deep sleep, the voice became louder and more urgent. When I opened my eyes I saw a man bent over my bed. He was in silhouette, kneeling at the other end of the bed, his elbows stuck out and his fingers outstretched as the hands moved together above the bed, as though he was looking for my neck. It appeared that he intended to strangle me. This was the realisation of my worst fear. Oddly, though, I felt no fear at all. What I felt at this moment was an unimaginably powerful feeling of love! The voice in my head ordered me, 'Scream! ... now, scream!' I struggled to manage a croak, and the moment I did, the intruder sprang silently to his feet and was gone in one graceful movement. In that instant the extraordinary feeling of love that had filled me vanished and was replaced by such a gripping fear that I began screaming in earnest and could not stop.

Two or three weeks after this I was coming home from work late at night and pulled into the driveway which I shared with another resident. The other car was not there so I drove my car to the bottom of the drive, which had a steep incline. The person who lived in the house in front of mine (I was at the rear of a 'battle axe block') had not yet come home. As I opened my car door to get out I noticed another car pull across the entrance to my driveway, blocking it off. The driver was staring at me strangely. Realising I could not reverse out of the driveway now, I instinctively got out of the car and walked up towards the gate that led into the front garden. The man in the car continued staring at me fixedly. I noticed a great disturbance in his eyes, he looked quite mad and was muttering under his breath.

Suddenly, his thoughts were telegraphed to me as if through a loudspeaker — he intended to kill me! As the realisation hit, a kind of anger rose powerfully inside me and a voice — mine this time, said calmly in my head, 'I will not be your victim.' Adrenaline and strength surged into my limbs, I was ready to defend myself and I knew I could do him a lot of damage. At the garden gate I stopped and looked penetratingly into his eyes. Quietly and calmly I said to him, 'I will remember your face. You have thirty seconds to get out of here before I call the police!' With that I turned and walked across the garden path, I did not run or panic or look back. As I turned the corner of the front house I noticed his car disappear up the road.

The police were not very interested in these incidents, and as a friend had commented to me after the first incident, it was, 'The LA wake up!' However, I knew now that someone or something was protecting me. The other thing that stood out was that I somehow felt lighter and freer. After the first incident, all fear of a thing like that happening left me completely. It had long been my worst fear.

Three weeks later I developed a very uneasy feeling at home one evening. Before going to bed I checked the locks and the windows several times. My house was now like Fort Knox with bars on every window and steel security doors, so I knew no one could get in. During the night I lay awake, vigilant. Countless times, I wandered through the house with the lights out to peer through the curtains. Though I saw nothing I could feel someone lurking out there under cover of the darkness, their 'vibe' was strong and menacing.

Some time before dawn, I fell asleep and was woken at about seven o'clock by a neighbour banging on the door loudly, calling my name. When I answered the door I saw fire engines, police cars and uniformed men milling around my next door neighbour's house. The street was blocked off. My front neighbour exclaimed, 'How could you sleep through all this? Sirens have been shrieking around here for at least an hour!' Then he paused and added, 'Alice has been murdered! She was murdered early this morning! I wanted to make sure you are all right.' Alice was our sweetly eccentric, harmless, eighty-year-old next door neighbour.

Shortly after Alice's death, a series of phone calls from Sydney prepared me for the imminent arrival in Los Angeles of someone called Brian who I had not met before. When he got in touch, we arranged to meet the following day at my place and drive out to Topanga Canyon, to a wonderful vegetarian restaurant for lunch.

All I knew about Brian was what I'd been told — he practised Raja Yoga, had some strong views on reincarnation and was coming to LA on business.

Brian was late arriving, so instead of driving out to the Canyon we settled for a place in West Hollywood. From the moment he set foot in my house I could feel there was 'something' about him that was very special, yet impossible to describe. He had a warm, easy nature and as the afternoon spilled away we talked and talked. He was an acutely intelligent person with much to share, especially on the subject of his spirituality. That evening I was late for a dinner appointment, unwilling to tear myself away from our conversation. Brian suggested we could go to Topanga Canyon for lunch the next day, but I was due to go to San Diego for the weekend and regretfully declined. As I dropped him off on my way to dinner, I was surprised to hear myself say, 'I'll cancel San Diego and pick you up in the morning, we'll go to Topanga Canyon for lunch.'

The canyon provides a peaceful, rambling encounter with nature, with its green undulating hills and valleys, spreading trees and unexpected glimpses of sparkling blue ocean. We walked deep into the canyon, then over lunch I told Brian about some of the recent 'occurrences' in my life. He listened attentively, appeared to consider all I was telling him and after a while, he offered his perception of these events. 'I think it means your karma is speeding up.'

'Why do you say that?' I asked. 'What does that mean?'

'I think you are about to go through some big spiritual change,' he replied. He saw my lack of understanding. 'Let me explain, I'll tell you about something that happened to me.' He proceeded to tell me how, as a driven and very successful high achiever in his field, he had been living in the fast lane for a long time. One night, driving well over the speed limit, he wrapped his car around a tree and was later pronounced dead. It was at the morgue that someone noticed a very slight movement of breath

12

playing on the sheet, covering Brian's face. His injuries were so extensive barely a single bone in his body was intact, he was rushed to hospital for surgery.

The accident stopped Brian in his tracks. He returned from the brink of death with an intense spiritual hunger, and the space to review his life. After being released from hospital he began looking into various spiritual groups. Eventually he encountered an organisation called the Brahma Kumaris, where he learned to meditate and, it seemed very apparent, found a home for his spiritual longings. It brought out the excited evangelist in him, he said, and he wanted to tell everyone, 'I've found IT!' Brian was hardly the evangelist–zealot type, but his enlightened perceptions and spiritual focus helped me make sense of things happening in my life then. I was hungry for more of his way of understanding.

By the time we returned to the meditation centre where he was staying, something had stirred in me. A few of his yogi colleagues were gathering to give him a farewell party before he left for the airport and quite a spread was laid out. He insisted I stay and meet these people. They were easy-going and friendly, and looked fresh in their spotless white clothes.

A week or two later I had a call from Mary, whom I had met at the meditation centre. She asked whether I had heard from Brian and invited me to the centre for dinner one evening. Delighted, I accepted and we arranged a night. As with Brian, the conversation was, for me, engrossing. I had connected with quite a few 'spiritual' people at a *satsang* (a spiritual gathering, which literally means 'in the company of truth') I'd been attending, but I had not encountered the depth or extraordinary perceptiveness that was evident in Brian and Mary. The next time I had dinner with Mary she invited me to have some herbal tea with her, which I drank as we chatted. At some point she asked me if I would like to join her while she meditated over the food. 'No,' I answered, 'I'm not into meditation.'

The meditation I had learned at the sat sang was, I concluded, a waste of time. It was also impractical, because I was supposed to be in a dark and soundless environment to do it. Meeting these requirements as much as one can in this world, I meditated and meditated persisting for many months — nothing happened! When I listened to people sharing their experiences at the sat sang I had no idea what they were talking about. Their sharing was esoteric, it was ethereal, but what exactly was this experience they said they were not able to describe? When Mary asked me to meditate, my resistance surfaced, surprising me as much as it did her. Her angelic face looked a little injured. The last thing I wanted to do was hurt her feelings, so to be polite I said, 'Okay, I will.'

She played a meditation commentary and I knelt on the floor. As my knees touched the carpet something extraordinary happened. I was no longer in the room, in fact, I was no longer in my physical body! I felt light as a feather as I was suddenly surrounded by swirling light, then colour — many different colours. I had a sense of travelling through light and the feeling was sublime. I have no idea how long this continued, but I was so present, so much a part of that experience. Nothing like it had ever happened to me before. In what seemed like an instant, it was all over and I was back in my body and back in the room. I looked across at Mary who was smiling at me, curiously.

'What did you put in that tea?' I asked.

That evening I asked Mary about karma. She explained some of the basic principles of the law of karma to me and for the first time, I was able to begin making sense of things that had happened in my life. She had a simple, very gentle way of explaining deep things. I left there that night on a bit of a high, but with a feeling of innocence, as though I was a tiny baby. I left with a feeling of fullness too, for I had received a valuable gift — the light of understanding.

ᎧᏬᏬ

There is a saying, 'What is yours will come to you.' In every aspect of life, I have understood this to be true, and so it is with spirituality. At the beginning we are innocents, we do not know the way. The trail markers that synchronicity or fate throw in our path are one way that 'something happens', but not the only way. For some it may be an emotional or physical or even a terminal illness that sets them on their path. While for others, like Brian, it takes a momentous or even life-shattering event to intercept their obsession with worldly goals and ideals. Then again, perhaps just simple, good old-fashioned curiosity draws us in. I believe each of us is given what we need, in precisely the way we need it.

Coming to know the self occurs entirely through awareness and experience. The depth of cognitive understanding comes later. Meditation facilitates an experience of soul, but there are many different practices and paths, and it is important for me to feel that whatever I am doing is right for me. The meditation I learned through the *satsang* was obviously preparing the way, but it was not where I was destined to land. Many paths do not have a body of knowledge or even a basic suggested practice. While this is just what some people find suitable, many others, like me, need a philosophy and a practice in order to develop spiritually. Ultimately, it is who I become through my spiritual practice that counts, not the philosophy itself, nor the prophet or guru. These are merely instruments to bring about transformation.

It seems no accident that the path of Raja Yoga presented itself to me once I had experienced something to compare it with. It is a path that suits me because of its inherent integrity, and also because there are no masters, no human gurus, no mantras, postures or breathing exercises — and there is no worship of human beings or even of God. It felt right for me. Raja Yoga nurtures and develops in me the ability to monitor and assess myself constantly, to find my own answers by understanding life in an unlimited way, and to be completely self-responsible.

Whatever each of us is meant to find seems to come and find us. Just as one two-year-old boy, of all the little boys in Tibet, was discovered and recognised as the Dalai Lama, our destiny will seek us out no matter how well hidden we are. Being open and receptive to that destiny is where the journey begins.

chapter two

TRUE IDENTITY

Our destiny is linked to the soul, but the soul must awaken to discover its highest destination. The question 'who am I?' becomes particularly relevant when our spiritual identity is forgotten. The journey to an enlightened state of being or total awareness, begins with the recognition that 'I' the soul, am not this body.

The journey of the soul has been compared to a game of hide and seek. This is because, over time, the soul gradually forgets its true spiritual identity, shifting increasingly to the outer identity of the body image, where it becomes lost and hidden from its self. The lost soul may quest for answers to the meaning of life, but only when we discover our true identity can we regain our wholeness.

We learn about our bodies at school and develop a growing sense of our physical identity and self-image from childhood onward. Similarly, getting in touch with our spiritual identity is based on an understanding of our spiritual form and nature. Coming to understand the soul is not just a theoretical exercise, not just 'head' knowledge. Meditation is important because it facilitates an experience of the *self* and, combined with some basic information about the soul, stirs and excites soul-awareness, which is something that may have ceased functioning long before you can remember. If you really want to understand the soul, I believe it is necessary to learn a meditation practice that focuses specifically on the soul. Meditation also opens the intellect so that we can comprehend and absorb spiritual knowledge.

As a soul, my primary relationship is with my self, then with the body. The roles I play in this life, and my whole identity is formed in conjunction with, and expressed through the body. However, 'I' am not this body. I, the soul, have this body. Interestingly, it is within this fundamental soul–body connection that the soul becomes separated from awareness of itself, undergoing a gradual shift to identification with the body. This loss of soul-awareness forms the basis of all human suffering.

The soul, and the physical form that embodies it are quite separate. Although I probably think of my physical form as 'me' it is really the soul that is 'I'. My body is created by my biological parents, but the soul does not come from the physical mother and father. While the foetus grows in the womb, the entry of the soul or life force takes place at approximately the end of the first trimester. Once the soul enters the fully formed foetus, the baby feels, senses and moves. From the time of conception the body goes through a growing and ageing process, culminating in a transition we term 'death'. At this time the soul leaves the body. Soul does not die, it is only the physical form, the body, that wears out. Thus, the spiritual essence continues whereas the physical form is temporary. Disidentification with the body and the physical roles in this life are part of the process of dying. Attachment to our own body, however, is so powerful it is probably the deepest attachment we experience in life.

While the foetus develops as a male or female, the soul itself does not have gender. Only the physical body has gender. As a soul is raised through the developmental stages from infancy and childhood to maturity, it is socialised and deeply conditioned to behave and express itself through its gender and physical identity. To become soul-conscious, which for me occurs naturally when I meditate and slip into my true awareness, means to transcend the limits and constraints of physical identity and social conditioning. Babies do not care about social conditioning or how others think they should behave. So innocent, free and natural are they that it is easy to appreciate the beauty of the unblemished soul.

Once during a long wait in a bank queue, I found myself in a line of workmen who, judging by their muddy work boots, must have been working on a building site in the area. A young mother with a baby about six months old was waiting in the bank near us, but not in line. The baby was wide awake and playful, making lots of baby 'talking' noises as it played and interacted with its mother. Soon, all of the men had turned in the baby's direction with their backs to the tellers, they were riveted. The tellers were having to shout to get the workmen's attention when their turn came to be served. The baby was oblivious to the attention it was attracting. Such is the natural beauty of the soul.

ဆုရငျ

Once we understand about our physical organs and what they do, bodily functions are easy to comprehend. In a similar way, the soul has organs that we use for our metaphysical functioning. These organs are: memory, intellect, mind, heart, conscience, awareness and will. The soul also feels, senses, and carries the subtle impressions or natural traits that make you a unique being.

Spirituality refers to my true essential nature. First and foremost, the nature of the soul is peaceful and non-violent. When my true identity is forgotten, my consciousness shifts from a soul-aware consciousness, and over time I move further away from my original nature of peace. But what precisely is my true identity? If the soul was observable, it would have the appearance of a tiny speck of light. This is what the soul is, a sentient being, just pure conscious energy, in the form of a nano-speck of light. Human eyes can see physical objects, but the soul is nonphysical, so it is not seen by physical eyes, under normal circumstances. The fact is, the soul cannot be seen, it can only be realised.

One way of understanding the soul is to think of a diamond. A soul possesses original qualities or divine virtues, which shine like facets of a diamond when revealed. Pure spiritual qualities never change, and in this sense may be described as eternal. They cannot be attained from another person or learned, as they only emerge from within. Our virtues are original, natural states of the soul.

As layers of personality gradually build up, encumbering the soul, our original virtues become covered up and their intensity diminishes. So many people want peace because they have lost touch with their natural state of peace. If they had not had peace to begin with, they would not feel the loss of it. The hunger for peace and spiritual connection attracts many souls to meditation.

When I begin to meditate, the first natural state or virtue I am likely to experience is peace. Peace is not something that I can get from outside myself. Even meditation does not 'give me peace', but when I meditate this action does connect me with the original state of peace that is inside, and has always been there. My original state of peace never deserts me. I simply forget that I am a peaceful being of light, and become disconnected from my essential state of peace. When I am in my original state of peace, this facet of the diamond radiates the vibration of my innate peace into the atmosphere. Soon the atmosphere in my environment will be imbued with peaceful vibrations. The power of soul-consciousness is such that it can transform the atmosphere in this way.

In its natural state of being, the soul experiences and emanates all of its divine virtues or original states of: *blissfulness, powerfulness, lightness, sweetness, peace, patience, compassion, purity, freedom, innocence, strength, beauty, benevolence, independence, unconditional love, truth, value, awareness, detachment, simplicity, creativity, spontaneity, equanimity, joy* and many more. These states of being are referred to as *super-sensuous* experiences, meaning 'beyond the physical senses'. For instance, *super-sensuous bliss* is not an emotion or a response to physical sensation, it springs from the soul and is a facet of our divine nature. This pure, virtue-filled self is our true identity. It is who we really are. The more soul-conscious we become through meditation, the more we experience and express our original divine virtues and our spiritual nature.

The soul-aware state is so pure and uncontaminated, that in soul-consciousness it is not possible to experience negativity or to project alienated parts of the personality onto others. So why is it that, instead of experiencing myself in this way, I experience anxiety, negative thinking patterns, anger, jealousy and depression? The reason is that I forget who I am, meaning my true spiritual identity; and when I forget I am a soul, I believe I am a body. In this way I begin to become separated from my true identity. As a young person growing up, my physical identity and the roles I take on become reinforced as my identity over and over again. This separation from self forms a layer of pain, loss and confusion at the core of my personality. The moment I lose my soul-aware consciousness the ego takes over. Ego is a kind of constructed 'self' that tries to mimic the true self. The ego develops as a way of fending off experiences of pain and discomfort, so it can be thought of as a defence mechanism or a

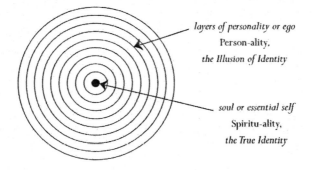

layers of personality or ego
Person-ality,
the *Illusion of Identity*

soul or essential self
Spiritu-ality,
the *True Identity*

Diagram I: *Identity*

shield. Ego is another term for personality. The most important thing to know about the ego or personality is that it is false. Over a period of time I forget my true identity and believe that the manufactured personality or ego is who 'I' am, which leads me to regard myself and the world in a false way.

When a human being is born the soul is in an emerged state. The innocence and purity of an infant reveals the natural state of the soul. Babies do not relate through the adaptation of personality, because they have not formed any ego defences or ego identity. In a world lacking spiritual vision and soul-awareness, an infant will not grow up with reminders of its spiritual nature. As a child grows and experiences little rejections and hurts, he or she gradually forms layers of resistance to avoid feeling the pain and disappointments that are a part of growing up in our world. Thus, the ego or personality begins to form as layers of 'protection' around the soul early in life. Two examples that illustrate how the spontaneity and joy of soul-awareness can be affected by our childhood experiences come to mind.

One pleasant winter's day I was walking on the beach. The weather was mild and there were two other people on the beach that morning. A young mother was with her daughter who looked about three years of age. The little girl ran into the water and squealed with delight, as though it was the first time she had ever seen the ocean. She danced at the water's edge, giving voice to high-pitched squeals of pure joy. As I walked by, the mother called to her child softly, 'Estelle!' The little girl swung around to look at her mother, still uttering her joyous cries. The mother bent forward, put a finger to her lips and said, 'sssshhhh'. I could hardly believe what I was hearing! Estelle's spontaneity and joy disappeared instantly, to be replaced by a look of shame. She looked crushed. Her shoulders slumped and she hung her head, looking down at the sand, convinced she had done something wrong. This reminded me of an incident when I was working with a theatre company in Scotland, many years before.

One hot summer afternoon, one of our principal actors was walking along the street with her two young children. Her children had recently arrived from London to be with their mother for the school holidays. Seeing a sprinkler on someone's front lawn, the children tore their clothes off and leapt under the sprinkler. As they ran to and fro under the spraying water, they shrieked and laughed with joy. Their mother, standing stock still in the road, stared at them for a full minute, silent and a little shocked. Suddenly, she threw her head back and laughed with an abandon and a freedom that matched her children's. The children laughed, ran and played under the sprinkler, then put on their clothes and looking bedraggled but happy, continued along the road with their mother.

Children are so easily crushed and so easily supported. A layer of hardness and resistance forms from the moment their openness and trust is dimmed and converted into mistrust and wariness. The real beauty and spontaneity of the soul is covered up little by little, layer by layer, year after year.

In one way these layers are an attempt to create some kind of insulation from external discomfort, but they also mask the soul. As these layers of personality increase and the outer identity is continually reinforced in daily life, 'I' experience a gradual change in consciousness. Eventually I believe that I am this body image, and I am the roles I play. For instance, I may see myself as a mother, a high achiever, a loser, someone who 'fixes' or takes care of others, or a person who makes everyone laugh. Hence my focus is always on the outer self, and on others. When I forget my true identity I experience a sense of deep loss and emptiness, which seems impossible to identify or articulate.

In his book *The Analyst and the Mystic*, a case study of the Bengali mystic and Hindu saint Shri Ramakrishna, Indian psychoanalyst Sudhir Kakar refers to, 'the depressive core at the base of human life, which lies beyond language.'[7] Kakar explores the idea that the potential mystic is better placed to connect with and possibly correct this depressive core, than a person in psychotherapy. To lose the true self is undoubtedly the greatest loss we can experience, as once this happens I depend on the environment (people, places and things outside myself) to let me know who 'I' am, to acknowledge me and make me feel good in a false way. Psychology, which actually means 'study of the soul', is a misnomer because psychology and psychologists deal principally with the personality and behaviour. While psychology may be empowering and effective in developing awareness at this level, it does not deal with the soul or transcend the false self.

The more I forget my true self, the more dependent I become on the environment for reassurance. The ego's need to feel acceptable is so great, that I begin to adapt behaviours and personality mechanisms to please others and society at large. Whatever it is that my society idealises and values, I will take on or perhaps oppose and rebel against. Either way the soul remains cut off and unnourished. Engaging with the world in a false way causes all kinds of problems that lead to much suffering. The more I live in a false way the more distant I become from my true self. Even after achieving important worldly goals I will still feel empty inside. Eventually a deep yearning develops within. It is difficult to describe or understand, but is a symptom of someone who is ruptured from their spirituality. There is nothing wrong with having material possessions, achievements, goals or fitting in with the status quo, but having been robbed of my true identity these outer things are a hollow substitute.

Once we recognise the difference between the true and false self, we have the power to choose which of these identities we express. Our true identity reveals us as divine beings of light — giving, uncomplicated and loving. Finding our true identity occurs through meditation, a journey into silence where the soul is released from the stricture of ego. Filled with lightness, virtues, and free as a bird — this is the soul, our true identity.

chapter three

ANATOMY *of the* SOUL

True identity is one dimension of the soul; our ego and associated behaviour add another dimension, but there is much more to the soul than this. Just as the body has its physical organs, the soul has its subtle counterparts — the spiritual organs or faculties — primarily: *mind, intellect, conscience, memory, awareness* and *will*, with which we *experience, feel, realise, discern, remember, express, think, comprehend, learn* and *act.* Our subtle faculties provide a third dimension to the soul, and to our existence. Imagine what would happen if one of our physical organs stopped working. The consequences would be life-threatening. If one of our spiritual 'organs' is impaired, however, this will probably go unnoticed, although the interruption to our functioning is just as serious. Sadly, a loss of spiritual function affects all of us.

A fully self-realised soul will experience one hundred per cent of its ability to use its subtle faculties, and can therefore function in a complete way. Such a soul gives full and free expression to its spiritual nature. If a spiritual function is blocked it is every bit as critical as kidney or heart failure, and just as threatening to our quality of life. Of course, we experience it in a different way: instead of the body collapsing, a part of our inner being will collapse. When spiritual function is blocked the body and mind eventually reflect this lack of self-support through mental, emotional or physical ailments.

Healthy maintenance of the soul is just as important as healthy maintenance of the physical body. The soul needs spiritual exercise, nurturing, attention and quality nourishment.

Meditation, spiritual knowledge, a balanced lifestyle and a way of living that integrates these are good ways of caring for the soul. This is why it is important to understand how our spiritual faculties work. The mind–body connection is so dynamic that a loss of physical function can have psychological consequences, or a loss of spiritual function can throw the physical system out of balance. In this way, reading the body and physical symptoms can lead to a greater understanding of the inner self.

Heart

The heart is our metaphysical feeling centre, and is directly linked to the limbic brain which governs our feelings and emotions. Neural pathways proliferate in the brain, but have also been discovered in the heart. All of our mental processes begin in the limbic brain which responds within point fifty of a millisecond to stimuli, delivering an emotional response which is felt in the body, as well as metaphysically. Neurobiological research has revealed that the emotion relays an impulse to the neo-cortex, which then produces a thought in our mind. The quality of our feelings and emotions is a major factor in deter-mining the quality of our thoughts and state of mind.

A significant link between the brain, lungs, heart, liver and gastrointestinal tract is the vagus nerve, a major nerve that travels from the brain stem and connects to all our organs. Via the vagus nerve, emotions directly affect our nervous system, heart, breathing, digestion, and all of our physical organs. Stimulation of the vagus nerve is now a treatment used for depression. In summary, everything begins with a feeling, which registers initially in the limbic brain, and is then felt in the body and mind.

Mind

Mind facilitates and creates thought, but does not exercise control over the quality of our thoughts. It simply manifests thought perpetually. A chaotic, rapid mind can be our worst enemy whilst a slow, deeply focused mind, is our best friend. The difference depends on several factors, including the quality of our emotions, and how well our intellect is engaged. A kind of child–parent relationship exists between mind and intellect. If the parent is working to ensure loving, attentive discipline, the child knows his or her limits, feels happy, and functions in a constructive manner. This is precisely the case with the mind. If the emotions are stable and the intellect is a watchful, effective parent, the mind will be well disciplined and relatively free of wasteful thinking. The mind that is free is available to apply itself powerfully and with great concentration to any given task.

An undisciplined mind thinks rapidly, is disorganised, unable to focus, and is swamped with waste thoughts. The mind in such a state is very draining for its owner and can be prone to anxiety. Problem-solving and concentration will be difficult. The mind uses the lion's share of our available energy, so when its power is constantly siphoned off by waste thought we become distracted, ineffective and exhausted. The undisciplined mind is also very vulnerable to repetitive thought patterns and sensory pulls of habits and addictions. In turn, these repetitious thoughts further disempower the mind, until in extreme circumstances they dominate it totally. Obsessive thinking and compulsive behaviour are the end result.

Not only do I think with my mind, I feel with a part of it as well. Mind tends to be associated with the left brain, but there is a connection between the mind and the heart —a powerful feeling centre. Painful emotions can destabilise the mind and impair mental function, whereas joyful feelings uplift the mind and dissolve mental and emotional barriers. While processing grief, loss and painful emotions is an essential part of living, feeling good promotes well-being and balance of mind and body.

Intellect

The function of the intellect is to analyse thoughts and focus the mind, enabling exploration of ideas and information in depth. The intellect harnesses the mind and is integral to our higher function. It is vital for problem-solving, mental tasks, creativity, learning and concentration. A strong intellect will control any kind of waste thinking, and inspires the mind to work creatively and constructively in all mental tasks. For many people, the intellect is a bit like a flabby, under-exercised muscle, with the result that it lacks power and control. Without power in the intellect to harness the mind, the mind rambles all over the place like an untethered horse. However, when we exercise the intellect with regular daily meditation, it begins to work better. Ultimately, the intellect becomes razor sharp, facilitating instant responsiveness and the very best performance the mind is capable of. This enables very deep, powerful, sustained concentration. The better the function of the intellect, the better the mind. Less thought will be produced because the intellect slows the mind right down. This saves valuable energy, which is then available for spiritual growth.

Conscience

The conscience acts as a filter through which our thoughts pass, prior to their being acted upon or expressed in any way. The conscience works in concert with the intellect and the will. It informs all of our actions, including our behaviour and speech. It speaks to us with a loud voice when it is working well. If I persist in acting against the voice of my conscience, I turn its volume down and will eventually sever the metaphysical 'nerve' that connects my conscience and my mind. When this connection is severed, my expression and actions can be considered to be out of control. An unmediated will becomes reckless. Severing the conscience has serious implications because the conscience also acts as a compass, a navigation or steering system, providing inner guidance and direction in all aspects of life.

By severing my conscience, I impair the integrity of the

intellect and will, and disintegration occurs. My actions can become hostile, wilful and antisocial. Without inner guidance, my life can become an undirected mess. The price of 'killing' the conscience is extremely high and restoring the metaphysical 'nerve' or connection between conscience and mind will be painful, initially. However, it is an unavoidable pain which promotes healing.

Memory

Our mind is conditioned by what we have already experienced and learned, whether conscious or unconscious. Each time we think, feel or act, an impression is left in our memory. The mind is not conditioned by the future or that which is outside our knowledge and experience. Hence, we need memory in order to function at most levels of our being. Without memory, the cognitive mind cannot function properly. As children we are socialised by remembering what it is we do that makes our parents and caregivers pleased or displeased with us. Impressions of our actions, speech, expression and experience are left in the memory to shape behaviour and functioning. From remembering how to do up our shoelaces as a small child, being praised for this (and feeling proud and empowered by this) to comprehending and interpreting vast amounts of information as a student, our memory is pivotal in enabling us to mature.

Memory is vital to our growth, and plays a central role in habit-forming, whether the habit is life-supporting or regressive. Deeply ingrained habits are caused by repetitive cycles of feeling — thinking — acting, in sequence, which are memorised over and over again. The sequence is repeated so often that the memory of it begins to have an unconscious, automatic effect on the mind and on our behaviour.

Repetitive patterns are referred to as addictions or compulsions. When addiction cycles form, they leach large amounts of spiritual power from the soul. Positive patterns and habits, such

29

as a balanced daily routine which includes meditation, exercise, good nutrition, play and taking care of responsibilities, provide strong positive memory impressions, enhancing feelings of well-being and inner power.

Awareness

Awareness is the *watcher watching*, the mirror in which I perceive exactly what I am doing and whether my actions come from my true self. With awareness I truly understand what it is I do, think or say that causes imbalance or suffering to myself or others. When the soul sees what the personality is doing, significant inner shifts follow. It is as though the soul and personality meet face to face at this point. The soul reveals the phoney behaviour to the personality that then experiences a deep repugnance for that behaviour. Such experiences are usually referred to as 'realisations', or an 'aha' and a flow of insight tends to follow. It is not uncommon to feel waves of relief and fulfilment after such a realisation. A great deal of energy that was bound up in the ego blockage becomes available for spiritual growth.

Following a realisation, blindness, ego-centred rigidity and deadness are replaced with spiritual insight and a feeling of being truly alive. Sometimes this experience is like an explosion. Often it is as though a kind of melting or dissolving of ego-defence takes place. These experiences can be profound, at times unleashing an intoxicating release of spiritual love. When we lose something that is false, our soul is able to emerge instead, restoring a feeling of wholeness and completeness. As transformation takes place I become more truly who I am. This is what real change is; a process of becoming more and more my true self as I continue to lose parts of my personality that are false.

Awareness is the instrument with which I monitor and work on myself. It is both the discriminating eye of the sculptor, and the sharp sculpting knife that cuts away whatever is covering up the natural beauty of the soul. With awareness, I can tune in to the important signals of the body, emotions and mind. Rather than blocking these vital messages, I can accept and work with them, developing insight. Tuning in to myself in this way is vital for self-knowledge and healing at physical, mental, emotional and spiritual levels of being.

Will

The will transfers thoughts, ideas, desires and needs into action. The will provides motivation, decision and the energy to act. When we engage the will we carry things out. Whatever we want to achieve requires the will to bring it into action. If we do not engage the will, desires and ideas remain unachieved. The will works in concert with the intellect and conscience that ensure integrity in our actions and expression.

When the metaphysical nerve that connects the will and the intellect and conscience is severed, there is nothing to mediate our actions. It is as if the will splits off and acts in a disaffected way. The will's involvement in our spiritual growth is essential. Meditation reconnects a severed will, bringing it back into working harmony with the intellect and conscience. It is important to understand that this is our natural state of being, and is a trigger for feelings of wholeness and completeness.

Meditation

By meditating regularly over time we continually attend to the repair and healing of our inner function and faculties. These in turn become highly activated in our feeling, thinking and acting in daily life. The more the conscience and intellect are engaged, the more integrated we become. As each thought or idea registers in the conscience, it is assessed as being congruent and in keeping with the true self, spiritual identity or spiritual purpose or not. At a refined level, anything not congruent with my true identity and purpose will be thrown out instantly. In this way I become very honest and straightforward in my expression and interactions with others. The conscience, intellect and will gradually work on clearing any backlog of 'items for processing' which have accumulated over time, thus helping the mind to become more free and light. In this way, I can resolve and let go of any past actions or events that may cause shame or distur- bance. I can also find it much easier to live with myself, as shadows and 'infections' within are cleansed and healed. With time and practice, my every thought, feeling, word, expression and action can be completely congruent and conscientiously connected to the true self. A pure lightness of being results, releasing a flow of bliss and contentment. Faith, a deep sense of confidence and empowerment, replace old postures of fear, anxiety, doubt and low self-esteem.

Intuition

Intuition is the voice of the soul, the quintessential speaker of truth. When the soul speaks, the message is compelling. The mind gives it absolute attention and is inexorably influenced. When we become alienated from our spirituality the intuitive voice is, to a large extent, switched off. However, just as the light of the soul can never be extinguished, the intuitive voice can never be completely silenced. It will speak, perhaps at the approach of a significant turning point in life, and it will be heard! The mind cannot block out or ignore this voice, because its truth pierces even the toughest constructions of ego-defence. The task of intuition is to reveal a truth that is pivotal to our growth, and at times our survival.

When I begin to change my consciousness through awareness of being a soul, I can tune in to a higher wavelength in my meditation and develop much better access to my intuition. Just as the third eye perceives the truth, so I develop a 'third ear', which dives beneath the static and chatter of the mind and penetrates the silence of the soul.

Once I develop my meditation to this point, my intuition and subtle faculties become more apparent, and become guiding forces in my life. As these aspects of the soul emerge and develop, spiritual growth becomes the purpose and fulfilment of life. All of this takes place very quietly and invisibly, within. Sometimes a divine voice may speak to us at a time of intense darkness and suffering. For the soul who is experiencing a massive dive into the torturous world of the 'inner void', this voice alone can pierce the darkness and abject isolation, bringing inspiration, hope and curiosity.

Awareness is the key, but of course I need all of my spiritual faculties to realise my potential and grow spiritually. The strange thing is, that if one of these functions becomes impaired, the others will too. Just as with the body, if the kidneys are not working well, there is a great strain on the liver and other organs. Likewise, if I sever my conscience or repress my memory or feelings, there is either an under- or over-compensating effect on awareness, will, mind and intellect. Meditation kick-starts the vital functions of the essential self and mobilises awareness. As meditation ignites the light of the soul it illuminates the darkness within, restoring the gift of insight and often triggering recovery of repressed memory.

Instead of this:

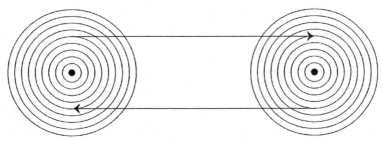

personality to personality

Diagram 2

I can relate like this:

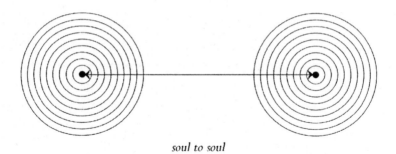

soul to soul

Diagram 3

Many people seek the serenity and peace that come with soul-consciousness in a variety of ways. Meditation is a balm for the soul, acting on our subtle organs, fine-tuning and bringing them into a state of balance and harmony. Feelings of wellbeing and centredness spring from this inner harmony and balance.

The soul is drawn to meditation because being self-aware is natural — it is just *being*. The original virtues of the soul are all experienced through meditation. The more I meditate on a regular daily basis, the more my natural state of being and original virtues flourish. Over time, consciousness also changes and the serenity and peace of the soul increasingly emerge. Meditation is very pleasant to experience and has a subtle, gently transforming effect. The more the soul emerges, the more the false personality recedes and dissolves. Day by day I become more truly who I am through consistent meditation practice.

Consciousness is like the energy space inside a balloon containing the 'furniture' of my spiritual organs, plus the sum total of my attitudes, values, beliefs, personality, coping mecha-nisms, world view, self-regard, innate functioning and awareness. It includes all of my behaviours, my conscious and unconscious programming; my drives, passions, practices, habits, integrity, emotions and nature. For instance, if I believe I am just a physical being whose existence finishes at death, the energy of my consciousness will differ greatly from someone who is attuned to their eternal spiritual nature. Transcending the material, mechanistic reality affects consciousness, which may contract or expand, accordingly. When I become attuned to all of the things about life which cannot be seen by the naked eye, or understood by ordinary logic and deduction, it is as though a door opens to another, more vast and mystical reality – the unconscious – or large mind of the true self.

An awakened consciousness easily grasps the paradox of destiny and free will, comprehends the natural laws and the eternal nature of things. A mystical consciousness is subtle, flowing, open, curious and receptive to what is. When I sit and meditate, my consciousness changes from the physical to the subtle. Over time, I will undergo significant and ongoing transformation.

The third eye is in the centre of the forehead, between the physical eyes. The people of India traditionally use a *tilak* or *bindi* to mark this energy centre. The opening of the third eye is facilitated through meditation. When the third eye opens, the gift of 'spiritual' or 'divine' vision is received. This means I am able to perceive myself, others and the world in an unlimited way from the perspective of the true self, rather than with the limited vision of the physical eyes. With my third eye I see the people around me as souls, instead of only seeing the body and relating to the constructs of personality, image and behaviour.

Relationships today are influenced so much by the ego-personality, it is little wonder people experience so much pain and confusion in this area of their lives. When my consciousness starts to change, I relate to others more from my true self rather than from my ego defences and acquired roles. This brings authenticity to my connections with others.

Seeing others as soul, rather than in the old way of seeing the body, brings a significant change of attitude. When a relationship takes place at the level of personality it is subject to the limitations of the ego. But imagine a relationship between two awakened souls who connect in elevated consciousness. This puts the relationship on a very different level, a level above the ego perspective of self and others that may oscillate from judgement and criticism, to putting people on a pedestal. When I connect with my innate spiritual value I experience deep contentment. I then see others in this way, too, and reach out to them with compassion and love rather than blame and criticism. In other words I do not learn to love myself and other people; it happens automatically when the soul is conscious and aware. We cannot learn the spiritual virtues or receive them from a teacher, but when our true consciousness is awakened they automatically emerge.

Once I understand the difference between the soul and the personality or ego, I can also understand the difference between feelings and emotions. Emotions may be confused with thoughts, as people often say, 'I feel' when referring to something they are thinking about. We do not think our feelings and emotions, we experience them. Emotions are reactive states which are produced at the level of personality as a result of stimuli from the environment or from thoughts. Because the personality is a phoney, defensive construct, our emotional reactions do not come from our true self. Becoming aware of our emotions opens the door to self-awareness and is vital for our personal growth.

Our feelings are connected to the 'original virtues' of the soul, which are sometimes referred to as 'essential states'. The essential state of love I experience is not the kind of love I experience emotionally. Essential love is a flowing of unconditional, unlimited, pure love. It is not directed to a particular person, it just emanates and flows from the heart. This is how the soul is — a flowing, emanating, pure being who is giving, benevolent and unlimited. In contrast, love as an emotion is conditional and has elements of attachment, neediness, dependency, control, desire and demands (in other words, 'I love you because ...' or 'I will love you if ...').

Often we say, 'I feel' this or that, yet the truth is that when the soul is really emanating compassion, the words 'I feel' are not used. Words are redundant when the soul expresses itself because our feelings are so powerful and clear. Feelings come from the soul's heart centre, whereas emotions come from the central nervous system and can cause mental imbalance. Feelings bring the mind into a state of centredness and positivity. Because they come from the soul, feelings produce a state of inner healing and balance. In soul-consciousness, it is impossible to experience negativity, whereas the emotions are largely negative and always reactive. For instance, I may feel triumph because I win an argument or joy when I win a lottery, but my joy is temporary and triggered by an external event.

Experiencing frequent negative emotions can make a person sick in mind and body. But true consciousness is automatically healing for the mind, body and spirit. Meditation brings me back into an authentic awareness of and relationship with the essential self — 'I' the soul.

In a nutshell, we have now explored three dimensions of the soul. The divine virtues endow the soul with its true identity and spiritual nature, which is the first dimension of the soul. In contrast to the true self, the false ego (which is created by the soul) with its defence mechanisms and associated behaviours, represents the second dimension of our existence. Our spiritual faculties or organs enable us to function as a sentient being, regardless of whether we are soul-conscious or ego-conscious, and represent a third dimension of our spirituality. (There is a fourth dimension of the soul, taken up in chapter eleven, which relates to our original spiritual powers.)

Finally, the purpose of meditation is to bring us into our original state of soul-consciousness so that we may experience the soul in contrast to the ego, and reclaim our true selves through the experience of *self-realisation*. The process itself is quite straightforward and the soul knows it is a simple matter, but the ego can feel extremely threatened by spiritual change, and may strongly resist the pull of soul-consciousness.

On one level, this means spiritual awakening can be a conflicted affair as the personality reinforces its position to 'battle it out' and defend against change. But on another level, the natural spiritual intoxication that suffuses the soul at a time of awakening, frees us to fly beyond, and transcend the influence of the false self.

chapter four

AWAKENING

Spiritual awakening heralds an unfolding of new life, a re-birth which follows a moment of conception and a period of gestation. This rite of passage is a silent yet profound moment, as the spirit is born from the darkness of ignorance into the light of awareness.

During the early days of my spiritual gestation, I made no secret of my cynicism about the existence of God. In April 1966 *Time* magazine had published an edition with an arresting front cover asking, 'Is God Dead?' I remember feeling shocked by this rearrangement of Nietzsche's statement, then pondering the question very deeply and clearly deciding that as the world seemed to be spinning so recklessly out of control, it had to be so. To make matters more complex, I had a deep mistrust of people who claimed any kind of authority to impart knowledge of God. This created an interesting framework for the experiences I was about to undergo.

Mary explained that the meditation centre would be going through some changes, as two people from San Francisco were moving in. She said one of them was a very experienced yogi and teacher and hoped that I would come and meet the new arrivals. This I did. Mary seemed to take a back seat after these two took up residence and I missed our evenings together very much. There was more activity at the centre as the new arrivals seemed keen to initiate new ways of connecting with the public. Where Mary was nurturing, gentle and very much in a heart space, our new teacher was sharp, tending to operate through her intellect. She had a great deal to offer and obviously enjoyed challenging, stimulating conversations, being especially adept at instigating them. Whenever I meditated with her, the room would fill with golden-white light. She was a dedicated yogi and obviously, a very powerful soul. I had been holding the Brahma Kumaris at a comfortable distance for quite some time and once she had this figured out, she decided it was time to push my boundaries.

One evening in August 1984, after spending some time at the Raja Yoga centre in an extremely provoking discussion, I decided conclusively that I was never going back! The discussion completely dissolved my comfort zone, leaving me in a disturbed and conflicted state. It was not the idea of a destruction of the current world order that bothered me, I had seen it coming for years. But the idea of time repeating in five thousand-year cycles, what an utterly arresting idea! It made so much sense, but my initial flash of insight and awareness was rapidly replaced by fear as I realised what this would mean for me.

'Exactly repeating cycles?' I asked. 'You mean I have to go through everything I've been through in my life all over again?'

'Exactly!' came the reply. 'You and I will sit here in five thousand years, on the same furniture, having this same conversation, wearing the same clothes, etcetera.'

'Thinking the same thoughts?' I added.

Suddenly, I wanted to reject what I was hearing. In fact, I wished I had never heard it — any of it!

As I drove home along Melrose Avenue knowing I would never go back, a heaviness crept into my body and I began to feel depressed. I was resolute in my decision and knew it to be absolutely final. By the time I arrived home my heaviness and feeling of depression had increased considerably. I felt so much discomfort that I pushed it all out of my mind and fell straight into bed. It was about 11 pm. At midnight something woke me and I sat bolt upright in bed. Actually, I was so wide awake and in a state of such heightened alertness that I noted how unusual this felt. The vibration in the room had changed, it was very still and silent. I felt myself drawn out of bed and into a sitting position on the floor. I then fell into a trance-like state of deep meditation.

After some time, I have no idea how long, something strange began to happen. I could hear a voice, which I recognised as my own. The voice was coming from my own subconscious mind and it sounded like a piece of magnetic tape being dragged across a sound-reading head, as happens in the film or sound-editing process. While I seemed to be observing what was happening, I was astounded at the questions I heard my own voice asking, because I was not consciously aware of these concerns at all. 'Why can't I have a relationship?' I heard myself ask. I must add that no one had told me I could not have a relationship. The answer came not from my voice but from another indescribable voice speaking in my mind. 'If you are in a relationship, ninety per cent of you is gone, which leaves ten per cent of you, and I want one hundred per cent of you.' Then my voice, 'Why can't I drink?' Then the answer, 'If you drink, that is sixty per cent of you gone, which leaves forty per cent of you. I want one hundred per cent of you.' The questions continued, and with each answer came the concluding statement, 'I want one hundred per cent of you.' Also, with each answer, the matter was brought to a close forever, as I experienced waves of love washing into me. I was in a state of hyper-awareness, unlike anything I had experienced before. So timeless was this event, that when I was released from the trance-like meditation, I realised it was not only broad daylight, but ten o'clock in the morning.

Night after night, I would again be awoken around the same time after very little sleep, then the interaction continued. Far from leaving me feeling tired, I cannot ever remember feeling so light, so clear, so present or so alive. For three weeks my feet did not touch the ground, and my consciousness was so altered I could not recognise myself. During this period I ceased using caffeine, nicotine, alcohol or anything that pulled me down from my blissful state. I remember eating mainly fruit. The joy and lightness of being was such, that I realised I had never known or even imagined true happiness in my life.

New faculties were opening up inside. Suddenly being able to see people's auras was one thing, but I was also reading their minds. The inner state of being of everyone I came into contact with, including complete strangers, was completely apparent to me. Yet none of this was occurring in a selective manner, I actually could not stop it. The silent fear I became aware of in others touched me, awakening a well of compassion. An energy centre in the region of my heart seemed to open, giving rise to a spring of love which flowed like a river. As I came in contact with people at work, friends, anyone at all, this love flowed from me and I would experience melting states of bliss, compassion, love and joy. Some time after the experience was over, I heard the term 'super-sensuous joy' and I knew this was the name for what I had experienced: joy beyond the senses.

During one of these 'sessions', I remember being shown some of my personality flaws quite clearly and precisely. The fact that this occurred without pain had quite an impact on me. I was surprised at the realisation of my own behaviour, but was neither hurt nor humiliated. Actually, I felt quite detached, yet eager to put things right. As a result, I was able to do some fast work on myself and quickly transform my offending behaviours. Until this happened I do not recall analysing any of what was happening. I simply lived in the moment the whole time, and accepted everything. However, I knew that under normal circumstances I would have been terribly hurt and angry with anyone who might point my faults out to me, a thought that lingered. This raised the question for the first time of who was 'doing it', who was communicating with me? Who could know me so well? Who was in my head all the time responding to so many of my feelings and thoughts? Who was this very definite personality

with such a dry, subtle sense of humour? Who could possibly know me so much better than I knew myself? Where was all this love coming from? For the first time my atheism was seriously confronted. There seemed to be only one answer, and feeling rather shaken by the obvious, I had to ask myself, 'why?' It just didn't make sense.

Since I had decided not to go back to the meditation centre, I kept all this to myself. Who was I going to tell, anyway? Who could explain it? Towards the end of these three weeks another strange experience occurred. It was much more than a dream that came to me one night. It was more like a vision, yet so vivid that I could not forget it.

I stood in the engine room of a ship, with twelve or thirteen other people. One of them I recognised as the captain, because he wore a blazer and a cap. The other passengers stood away from me in a bit of a huddle, and I could feel their cold stares and whispers. I felt isolated from the group. Every now and again one of the passengers would come over to me, only to give me an intense berating. One by one they came, as I tried desperately to catch the eye of the captain, without success. Finally, after they had all berated me, the captain approached me and began to do the same. I quickly looked around for an escape route, but there was none, not even a porthole. Suddenly everything went black and I could hear the voice of a friend calling me through the darkness, 'Over here, follow me.' I ran towards the voice and found myself running up a flight of steel steps behind my friend. It was pitch black and all I could hear was the clatter of our high heels on the steps. Up and up we climbed, for what seemed a very long time, in the dark. Eventually, my friend's voice said, 'Open your eyes!' I did so, to find I was way above the Earth in space, with a little blue pearl far below and a microscopic ship on the ocean's surface. I was alone. Then the voice spoke, but it was no longer the voice of my friend, it was the voice which had been communicating with me over the past weeks, 'Look, now do you see?

This is where you should be, up here with me, not down there with them.'

This vision continued, just like a movie:

Suddenly I was at my mother's front door in Sydney. The door was closed and as I stood in front of it, the door opened as though by magic. No one was there. I moved inside slowly, noticing a very different vibration in the place. Clearly, the house was empty. Very slowly I wandered through into my old bedroom and as I entered, the room opened out into the most indescribably beautiful, luxuriant, tropical garden. Filled with wonder, I wandered right into the garden, spellbound by the peace and beauty. I seemed to be alone, until I noticed three extremely subtle presences approaching. They were souls, and their form was so light and subtle I seemed to sense them with my third eye. They moved it seemed, on air, and their presence was feminine, in fact funnily enough, they reminded me of the three sisters at the meditation centre. They invited me, telepathically, to have a shower. I thought this was a little odd but a shower appeared before me and I stepped into it. As water began to fall on my head I found myself away from my body, watching. As water fell, the top of my head became white and then gradually, the whiteness spread downwards, all the way down my body to the tip of my toes. At last I was a gleaming white light, all of me, absolutely glowing. I stepped out of the shower and was instantly in a change of scene. Now I was on a wharf, staring at the ship. As I stared the other passengers and captain came out on the deck, staring back at me in disbelief for a long time. Eventually they walked in a single file down the gangplank, forming a circle around me on the wharf. One by one, I looked at each of them in their third-eye point, and as I did so, they too became pure. As each one turned completely white, I moved on to the next until all of them were pure.

At the conclusion of this vision or dream, I was absolutely awake and alert, feeling wonderful, but I had a big question mark in my

heart. What did it mean? What was all this about? My frame of reference and past conditioning were of no use to me at all. This was way beyond the boundaries of my limited existence, and curiosity plagued me. When the phone rang early in the morning, it shook me from my reverie. It was one of the sisters from the Raja Yoga centre inviting me to come for dinner that evening as Sister Jayanti (Director of BK international operations in London) was to be there. I had met her on two occasions. Jayanti was an extremely experienced yogi in a prominent position within the organisation — which is administered entirely by women — and possessed a wonderful ability to 'meet' others on an equal and warmly human level. She was about the same age as me and very 'Western' in her thinking and presentation, having been educated in London. The timing of her visit did not elude me. I accepted the invitation.

All evening I was torn between the determination not to tell them about my experience, for fear it might indicate I was 'one of them', and the implacable desire to get an explanation. Naturally, I was confident they would know what it all meant. I sat right through the evening without saying a word about any of it. Just before Jayanti left to catch a flight back to London, I told her. She listened with great interest, but said nothing. 'Well,' I asked expectantly, 'what do you make of it?' 'It's wonderful, Judi,' she smiled warmly, in her clearly modulated voice. 'Is that all?' I responded, wide-eyed. Seeing my perplexity she began to laugh. 'Yes, that's all,' she replied quickly, 'you'll figure it out!' It occurred to me that somehow, she had me 'figured out'. Interesting, I thought, when I couldn't even figure myself out!

Weeks later, I was still no closer to figuring it out, and sought an explanation from one of the sisters at the meditation centre. 'You just need a spiritual shower to become pure,' she said, 'your karma is changing!'

ᎦᏍᎦᏢ

The honeymoon lasted for two years. Despite the powerful attraction that was gently engaging me, my resistance continued. 'You are in the spiritual closet!' someone from the centre charged me, causing me considerable embarrassment. I was afraid I would be ridiculed if people knew what I was doing. My closest friends were privy to my visits to the centre and began to make frequent observations that I had changed, though they 'could not put it into words'. Two of my friends knew the whole story and seeing me change in a short space of time, became curious themselves. As I grew less neurotic and tortured about not being an atheist, I was able to open up to more of my friends and eventually, many of them came along to check out the meditation centre. As it turned out, no one ridiculed me.

Most powerful of all, I was getting to know the nature and personality of the Soul who seemed to be in almost constant connection with me. Around this time an actress friend gave me a kitten for my birthday, which I was far from happy about. I refused the gift as I did not want to be responsible for the kitten. 'Please Judi, just take her home for a night and see if you like her!' she exhorted, 'she was born in the theatre!' 'I can't just take her home for a night, I'll get attached!' 'The theatre manager will have her put down if I take her back to the theatre. Please Judi, just take her home!'

The tiny grey and white fluff ball became known as Mattie, short for Matilda. She had hardly taken up residence when one morning at almost four o'clock I felt a little thud on my face, then purring, and little paws patting my face. I got out of bed and gave her some milk, but she was not interested. When I returned to bed she jumped on my head. Little paws patted my face again, and she made some little miaows. This kitten meant me to get up! I was determined not to! However, she continued dive-bombing, patting my face and miaowing. Eventually, in desperation, I got up and meditated, while she sat contentedly in my lap, purring loudly. At four am the next morning and thereafter, the same thing happened. No matter how tired I was, thud, she was relentless. It occurred to me to wonder who was motivating the behaviour of this seven-week old kitten.

Around this time I was doing some casting for a film. To this end, I found myself one evening in a club in a rather dangerous part of Los Angeles, watching ethnic stand-up comedians. The hour was late and the place was packed with people, most of whom seemed several feet taller than me. I felt about elbow height squashed in amongst the crowd. The onstage work was excellent and the audience was having a good time. At the break I realised I was going to have to forge my way through the crowd to get to the other side of the stage, where I had arranged to meet some of the performers. It was very dark in the club and as I pondered whether the lights might come up or not, I noticed a woman elbowing her way through the sea of people. She was an extremely beautiful black woman. As she approached me somewhat breathless from pushing her way through the crowd she searched my face eagerly. 'I've been watching you from the other side of the room ever since you arrived, I just had to come and speak to you,' she said, 'even from that distance you stand out like a beacon. You look like a person who has found all the answers!' I was absolutely stunned.

These experiences indicated to me that the soul who had entered my life had a deeply intimate knowledge of me yet was never intrusive. This Being possessed an endearing nature, and a sense of humour! Most importantly, I recognised that this whole scenario had not been facilitated by another human being. I would never accept God through a human being, but how could I deny my own experience?

Something important was taking place, a new kind of learning that comes about through experience and through another inner process that I will attempt to describe. One morning I woke up and sat bolt upright as a huge realisation hit me. It was to do with the spiritual information I had been hearing all this time. It was as though my inner computer had been checking it all out subconsciously and had suddenly completed the job. 'It is all true and all your conditioning is false!' was the message from within. It was like being hit with a sledge-hammer! My whole world view was completely shattered. The shock was not just cognitive, I could feel it in every cell of my body.

Of course, I realised this confirmation was what I had been dreading. If the BKs were right, this meant I was 'responsible' for myself in ways I preferred not to think about. I was responsible for my own existence! How much longer could I hold all of this at arm's length, including the BKs? Certainly, I was not the type to surrender without a good fight and I was not ready to hang out the white flag yet.

An interesting twist of fate occurred around this time. I received a phone call from someone at the satsang, asking if I would be the production manager for one of their large public events. Though I had not attended their gatherings for a while, I was happy to oblige. I attended the production meetings, impressed by their slick organisation and dedication. The event was to be a talk by the guru, whom I had not met and knew nothing about, at a large, elite and very expensive venue in LA. The production meetings revealed something I had not come across at the satsang. It began with someone saying they would carpet the backstage toilet, scrub the whole booth and toilet out with a toothbrush beforehand, and replace the seat with a gold one, for the guru's use only! Since we were using a five-star venue this came as a shock, it was hardly a run-down church hall, but there was more. Their devotional, worshipping tones were letting me know these people had some kind of extraordinary deified projection on the guru. Surely they do not think he's God! I thought to myself, repelled by the idea. I kept my thoughts to myself and observed and listened.

The big day arrived and every seat in the auditorium was

filled. Everything went off like clockwork, without a hitch. The only thing was, where was the guru? Two thousand people sat there. We waited for well over an hour, before being told his limo had arrived. Eventually, a smartly dressed man walked on stage and sat down. There was a hushed silence as he launched into his talk, without any explanation for his lateness. He spoke quite impressively for about an hour, with the slick finesse of a trained presenter, it seemed to me, rather than the humility of a spiritual leader. At the end of his talk, he requested questions from the audience, reminding us that if we wished to make a speech we should rent the venue ourselves, rather than make speeches at his expense! I was sitting in the centre of the front row and had only one question to ask this fellow, so I raised my hand, along with many others. He selected me. A radio microphone was quickly brought to me and I framed my question with care. 'Guru ... do you see yourself as an instrument of God?' Then I waited, curious for his reaction.

There seemed to be a shocked silence in the room following my question. He paused, his eyes widening as he stared at me, then answered the question by way of an attack, which brought loud applause and cheers from his devotees. For twenty minutes his voice carried shrilly through the room. Initially, I felt horribly embarrassed, but this quickly passed as I got a grip on the situation, realising why this was happening. It was for my benefit. As he took more questions the situation became more and more clear. The guru's event coordinator stood up to say, 'Guru ... I don't love you any more. How is it that I could have felt such love for you ... and now ... I don't?' 'That's your problem!' he was told sharply, more cheers and applause. At the end of the day none of the production team spoke to me, with the exception of the coordinator. He crossed the room to find me and took both my hands in his, 'I'm so sorry that happened to you,' he said 'but that question had to be asked, thank you for asking it!' I told him that I had learned a great deal from the whole experience, and that it was meant to be. 'And where are you with all this?' I asked, curious. 'I have a lot to consider, as you can see.' 'Yes, I rather had that impression,' I responded, and wishing him well, I left.

Walking back to the car I felt the sun on my back and a breeze on my face as a lightness and freedom began to fill me. White, fluffy clouds surrounded by blue, scudded playfully across the afternoon sky. I gazed into the sky, then at the trees lining the wide street and they seemed more green, the sky more blue, the clouds more white, the colours around me more vivid. Everything seemed more alive. Actually, the world felt different. I felt as though, in the company of falsehood, I had gained a tiny bit of real understanding that afternoon. The clarity and truth of my own recent experiences stood out in sharp relief now, as did the love, the gentle humour and humility of the Soul who spoke to me in my dreams, my visions and my mind.

The genuineness and humility of the BKs also stood out, relative to the guru, and I felt warmly drawn to their simplicity. Their organisation of public programs was not slick like the guru's team, but it was heartfelt. I smiled to myself as I remembered a Raja Yoga program several weeks before, when the audience were sent to the wrong venue, and the mortification of the person responsible. That day was saved by some quick thinking. Afterwards everyone laughed about it and it was never mentioned again. Donations at the end of the guru's program must have totalled a grand sum, as big notes and large cheques were crammed onto huge collection trays. At the end of a BK program, usually held in a simple venue, the donations (which were unrequested) would have rattled around in a small tin. A very warm feeling filled my heart as I crossed the parking lot. This had been an interesting day!

chapter five

the SUBTLE
ENCOUNTER

Soul-consciousness prepares the way for the next stage of meditation that happens automatically and has similarities with a curious human experience that has been well documented over the past five decades. In Raymond A. Moody's book *Life After Life*, the 'Being of Light' in people's near-death experiences is referred to frequently and is described as an encounter with a very bright light.

> *Typically, at its first appearance this light is dim, but it rapidly gets brighter until it reaches an unearthly brilliance ... not one person [who has experienced this] has expressed any doubt whatsoever that it was a being, a being of light ... a personal being ... [with] a very definite personality. The love and warmth which emanate from this being to the dying person are utterly beyond words, and he feels completely surrounded and taken up in it, completely at ease and accepted in the presence of this being.*[8]

My own encounters with 'The Being of Light' in meditation fit very comfortably with the experiences that Raymond Moody describes. The soul who has 'died' and the soul in meditation have a lot in common it seems, when it comes to the subtle encounter. Entering this encounter through meditation means dying in a different way. It means dying to my own thoughts, senses and the pulls that so easily interfere with the delicate connection between two souls, for such a connection requires steady focus and a stable mind. Dedicated practice seems to be the way to achieve this. A direct relationship with the 'Being of Light' is what the next stage of meditation is all about. Once the movement into soul-consciousness is achieved, attraction to the Being of Light is the next step.

Meditation is the way of connecting with this Being, who is without gender, sensory faculties or physical presence. Developing a deep and subtle relationship with this Soul, through the mind, is what enables the human soul to be restored to full awareness. The original fullness, completeness and power of the soul is regained in this way. This second stage of meditation is called yoga, which means 'union' and is a way of connecting spiritually. Yoga brings deep sensations of peace and super sensuous bliss, whereas dealing with an intellectual understanding of God poses one of the most controversial issues in the spiritual arena today. Spiritual knowledge that opens the soul to new awareness can be very exciting, but also very challenging. New perspectives are not gained from standing in the comfort zone of old ideas. Somehow, when the soul wants us to grow, it seems to have a knack of pushing us out of our 'thinking square' and into places where exposure to new influences take place. The ability to keep an open mind and suspend judgement is invaluable, especially when the ego is feeling threatened.

Most of what I have come to understand spiritually has dismantled much of the conditioning and programming I have been exposed to in my life. I have no regrets about this, as the deprogramming through meditation and higher knowledge has brought so much clarity and relief. Developing a construct of and relationship with a Higher Being is very personal. The insights and understanding I share are no less personal.

The soul is the life force and the inner light in a human being. It has knowledge that it does not necessarily share with the conscious mind. When we begin to understand how the ego works, this can seem an act of divine wisdom. However, when soul wants us to know something, it will make sure we get the message. Like the Being of Light, human souls are infused with spiritual light or power, which energises the life force. When spiritual power diminishes, the soul's light also dims and insight disappears, inner darkness grows and weariness pervades. Because the soul is eternal, the inner flame can never be extinguished. There is no such thing as actual spiritual death but there is a kind of rock bottom. Feelings of emptiness, deadness, exhaustion and lack of vision characterise spiritual burnout in a human being.

Replenishing the spirit involves entering the spiritual dimension. The physical dimension, with all of its sciences and healing arts that are wonderful for the physical body, cannot bring about spiritual renewal. Through meditation, the soul, having first become soul-conscious, may move naturally and automatically into connection with the Being of Light. Rather like the prodigal child returning, the impoverished, fully spent soul returns to the warm embrace of the spiritual Mother and Father to experience pure love and sustenance once more. The Being of Light is untouched by the spiritually erosive influences we who have a physical identity are subject to, and free from the fluctuations and emptying of spiritual power that we undergo.

As tiny points of light, we are created 'in His image', which is not physical but in the form of light. Relationship is at the very heart of spiritual growth. Unconditional acceptance, regard and love enable the soul to flourish and grow. Who can know me beyond the limits and self-centredness of the personality? Who can look beneath the well-constructed armour I hide behind and see me only as an exquisite and divine being who has simply lost her way? Who else can reveal my true identity to me?

Many aspects of religious training and education work to sever the soul's relationship with a Higher Being. As a result spiritual allergies are commonplace. A fearsome, punishing God is hardly the image I want to warm my toes by, let alone trust with my heart and soul. Many ideas about God simply contribute to the rupturing and separation that many souls experience, whereas a loving relationship is the birthright of all. To have access to a relationship with God without an intercessor, without dogma, without judgements or shame, and without financial cost is a basic human right. Any spiritual knowledge or spiritual path that comes with a set of fees and conditions cannot be pure. True knowledge and a direct and exclusive relationship with God, is available for everyone and it is free.

Up until the 1950s and 1960s, religious education taught us that God was in Heaven, which was up in the sky. Somewhere between then and the end of the twentieth century, God apparently moved and is now 'everywhere'. The omnipresence dictum (the idea that God is everywhere and in everything) originates in the *Bhagavad Gita* (the scripture of India) and has infiltrated the West since the 1960s. Omnipresence is now accepted religious teaching in the West and is generally embraced uncritically. However, if God is supposedly everywhere and in everything, this means She is involved in every perpetration of atrocity, violence, rape, murder, paedophilia, torture, arson, oppression and terrorism. It means God is also a victim of all of the aforementioned things, as well as being in all the nuclear weapons, drugs, firearms, alcohol, poisons, contaminants, garbage and pollutants that are destroying the Earth's environment. How can a perfect, benevolent, unconditionally loving, powerful and creative force be these things? How can the 'Being of Light' that the dying person comes in contact with on the 'other side' be everywhere? The sun has its position in the universe and its light and heat are experienced everywhere, but the sun itself is not everywhere, it is located in one place. Omnipresence may pose a comfortable retreat from the fire and brimstone approach of Christianity, but closer examination of this concept highlights many irrationalities. The power of a widely accepted view is such that people blindly take it for granted and do not question it. The seeker of wisdom and truth, however, feels the need for deep questioning.

ço

The human eyeball is a small organ of such amazing complexity and wonder, that the idea of a couple of cells mutating in a swamp zillions of years ago and ending up a random adaptation called *homo erectus*, while certainly an interesting hypothesis, has been accorded unwarranted credibility given that it has never been scientifically proven. Medical science has made massive leaps, but it cannot create an eyeball, let alone a nervous system. Having blind faith in information that comes from a book or another person is one kind of faith, but there is another faith that comes from knowledge gained through experience. The addict who surrenders her addiction to a Higher Power, with the result that the compulsion to use a substance is miraculously removed, develops faith on the basis of a phenomenological–spiritual experience. The cognitive awareness of faith that arises from this, comes from the intellect. This is the other kind of faith — faith in the intellect.

Giving up the idea that human beings are God may well be one of the greatest challenges of our time. Humankind has played at being God for so long, and while the human race is capable of great accomplishments, the knowledge that we are not God is what keeps us compassionately and humbly in touch with our fallibility, limitations and humanness. Being able to turn to a Power greater than and separate from the self, through prayer, meditation, or thought — when the setbacks of life overwhelm, plays a significant role in people's ability to find forbearance, hope and healing. The power of prayer, meditation and positive thinking on people in a variety of helpless and critical situations is today well researched and needs no intro-duction.

Being in relationship and in communication with another identifiable soul that we can know intimately, connect with, relate to and experience is personal, but trying to be in a deep, loving and intimate relationship with a completely deperson- alised omnipresent 'everything, everywhere' is neither practical, logical nor realistic. When the human soul has become very caught up in misguided ideas and has not even approached a real relationship with the self, this notion of omnipresent relationship is confusing rather than healing.

Healing our relationship with ourselves and with the 'Being of Light' is where our spiritual purpose lies, it is the soul's path to wholeness. Attachment to making lots of money, falling in love, owning beautiful and expensive possessions or chasing power, achievement and fame are the predilections and obsessions of the personality. Like playing God, these are the pursuits that empty the soul of its truth, and lead us down the wrong track. Getting on track with ourselves spiritually is not something we do alone, we need the 'subtle encounter' to be reminded and to bring us back to who we are.

Transformation involves spiritual effort and spiritual effort brings rewards. With regular practice of meditation over time, I began to notice small changes in myself. Initially, I noticed I was less irritated by things which would have angered me a matter of days ago. Tolerance seemed to be replacing irritation. After a while, I noted a growing distaste for certain behaviours in myself. It was as if the real me was returning.

Meditation sharpens the intellect like a razor, and as discrim- ination increases it begins to transform the personality. Quite quickly, spiritual power begins to inform actions, decisions, and connections with others. The more spiritual power is accumu- lated, the more effective we become. Habits and regressive behaviours change, as entrenched ego defences gradually dissolve.

The one thing people who have 'died,' most commonly

express enormous regret about when their lives 'flash before their eyes', are the times in their life when they withheld love. Great importance is attached to forgiveness on the spiritual path because resentments, whether they are trivial or whether they stem from deeply traumatic wounding experiences, penetrate deeply into the psyche, creating immense blockage to spiritual growth. Resentment, described by Fritz Perls as 'the bight that hangs on',[9] more than any other ego defence, entraps us in guilt, blame and anger. Resentment is not healed at the level it is created or experienced, for it is the spirit that transcends and forgives. Moving into soul-consciousness allows such a different perspective, it facilitates our natural ability to let go. All souls are responsible for their own actions and must experience the karmic return of their actions. Forgiveness does not erase or negate responsibility, but it does open the floodgates, unblocking the flow of spiritual love and healing. Making amends to those we have injured intentionally or unintentionally, and forgiving those who have injured us, brings the soul into a state of liberation. The freer the spirit, the more freely it moves into the subtle encounter and into the blessed state of communion.

'What have you done with your life that you want to show me?' In Raymond Moody's *Life After Life* so many dying people have reported being asked this question by the 'Being of Light'. It seems a relevant question to ask ourselves right now.

chapter six

the SOUL *and the*
NATURAL LAWS

When the soul takes birth it enters what is sometimes referred to as 'the field of karma', which means the physical world where the soul interacts with matter. Just as the rules of the road or the laws of our country are designed to let us know the boundaries within which we may safely and lawfully conduct our lives, the natural laws play a similar role, governing our actions in the world of matter.

My friend Laurie and I were walking along the beach as we always did whenever I drove down to visit her, when a young woman stopped us to ask a question. A conversation followed and after about ten minutes we continued on our respective ways. As we walked on Laurie commented, 'You know Jude, I wonder if she is a new soul, or an old soul with great karma?' 'Why do you say that?' I answered. 'Because she's so beautiful. A new soul has no negative karma so they will get a really lovely physical vehicle, or an old soul with very good karma will too. I wonder which she is?' 'Are you saying that we get our body according to our karma?' 'Yes', Laurie replied, 'in India they say that very benevolent or philanthropic actions create a beautiful physical vehicle in the next birth.'

Oscar Wilde's classic, *The Picture of Dorian Grey*[10] provides a wonderful metaphor for the effect of action on the human soul. The actual portrait of the extremely handsome young Dorian symbolises the soul. The outcome of a deal Dorian has made with the devil means that each of his hurtful and vicious actions towards others leaves a faint impression on the portrait. Initially the effect is subtle, as Dorian notices a barely discernible hardening around the mouth in his portrait, but after a short while the mouth begins to look cruel so he removes the picture from view and stores it, covered in his attic, where no one may see it. His occasional forays into the attic reveal grotesque disfigurement and premature ageing of the once extraordinarily beautiful face in the portrait, as Dorian's narcissism, arrogance and cruelty continue to escalate.

The natural laws are telling us precisely this, that each of our actions leaves an impression in the soul, so that the quality of our past actions can be seen in the quality of our life and relationships in the present. Simply put, the quality of our past and present actions dictates the quality of our life. Loving, benevolent actions will come back to us, just as selfish, angry actions will. The natural laws operate like a magnetic force which completely supports spiritual development. These laws explain why awful things happen to 'good' people, and why good things happen to 'awful' people. They make sense of what may otherwise seem a set of random, inexplicable and senseless events. They help us understand why life is the way it is. Most importantly, these laws teach us how to get real control of our lives and how we can alter the course of our destiny. Understanding how these laws (also known as karma) work is truly empowering.

The law of karma, which simply means 'action', defines the magnetic force of energy that propels us into connection with people, places and situations in order to equalise our accounts. It also defines the force that works through magnetic repulsion, sometimes separating us from those people, places and situations once the account is settled. Two factors determine the effects of the natural laws on the soul: action and attitude. The intention behind any action is what creates the account, be it negative, positive or neutral. The deepest nature of the soul is to express itself, to be in relationship, and to perform action. These things can only be accomplished through the body. Without a body the soul is unable to interact with matter. The natural laws teach us that whatever we think, feel, do or say has consequence.

The energy of karma is the most powerful force that governs us. It reflects our actions and the attitude with which we perform those actions, back to us. The Bible sums it up thus: 'For whatsoever a man soweth, that shall he also reap.'[11] Newton's Law of Relativity also defines the natural laws: 'Every action has an equal and opposite reaction.' However, the law of karma was enumerated two and a half thousand years ago in the Indian scriptures, which have been around much longer than the Bible or mechanistic theory. The natural laws govern our existence on the physical plane and influence our lives profoundly. To gain a deep comprehension of these laws is to gain control of our life and destiny. Understanding the natural laws means we not only have the power to turn our life around, but also have the power to alter the course of our fate.

As a soul in a body, I have to perform action constantly to survive. Karma simply means 'action', yet actions are always performed with intent and attitude. According to the attitude and intention with which I perform any action, that action may either return to me in a beneficial way, a distressing way or in a neutral way. This is the law. No one is exempt from the natural laws of cause and effect. Every time I have a thought, a feeling or perform an action, this law is working. For instance, if I have a negative thought and develop that into an hour or a morning of negative thinking, that negativity will return to me. As a result I may feel depressed or angry, end up with a headache, a lowered immune system, low energy and have the kind of day I would rather forget.

My thoughts affect matter and other people, as well as me. Thoughts also affect the environment. Children and animals are very attuned to the vibrations of others. They may go spontaneously to a total stranger or keep their distance from someone well known to them. Someone once told me they did not trust a certain person. When I asked why, they replied, 'Because the dog doesn't like him!' Tuning in to someone's 'vibe' means picking up on the quality of their energy. A person with a 'good vibe,' will come from a place of positivity and caring, and have an attitude and presentation congruent with this; whereas a person with a 'bad vibe' may be holding a lot of anger, resentment or arrogance in their thoughts and attitude.

Our thoughts influence and shape our personality and physical wellbeing in an obvious way. If there is tension or anxiety in the mind, it will undoubtedly be reflected in the body.

Our thoughts affect us emotionally and physically. They also affect the atmosphere. Learning to monitor thoughts using the faculty of 'awareness' facilitates the ability to change your thinking. Meditation awakens awareness. When you catch yourself pursuing a train of thought that is taking you in a downward spiral, you can talk to yourself and pull yourself out of it. If you decide to perform an action that is motivated by anger, jealousy, hatred or resentment, remember this is what will come back to you. Doing something kind and caring for your enemy will help to defuse the situation between you and them. Maintaining a posture of retaliation or aggression with another means feeding a regressive situation that will rebound in an intensified way. If you refuse to maintain a posture of aggression towards another, he or she will not be able to maintain it towards you. Remember, it takes two to create a conflict. Mohandas Gandhi's understanding of the natural laws was intrinsic to his way of freeing India from British rule. His strict policy of non-violence and passive resistance was guaranteed to bring victory according to the law of karma, and of course it did.

While the natural laws can have a very intricate effect, they are essentially quite straightforward. There are two qualities of action: impure and pure. All action has an effect so there is no neutral karma, but if you imagine a continuum between pure and impure, the midpoint will represent the least effect. The attitude that motivates action is the determining factor. If I do something that is intended to benefit another person and it backfires, there will not be a negative rebound because my intention was pure. However, if I perform an action intended to hurt another person and for some reason it does not turn out that way, I will still get the rebound I set in motion.

Equalising the energy of action occurs in several ways: for example, through the physical body, the mind, finances, possessions, time and relationships. We also settle accounts when we have so-called 'accidents' or through the natural elements in manifestations such as droughts, floods, earthquakes, tsunami, storms, volcanoes, extreme heat, cold and other 'natural' calamities. The suffering experienced through any of these factors is the actual settlement of the account. Impure accounts of action are settled by suffering. Ultimately, it is not possible to avoid settling an account. Accounts usually present in quite a small way initially, so that if I have humility and sensitivity I will recognise the situation and settle it. If I ignore the account, it will snowball and present itself in a larger form later. As long as I dodge the account, it will keep snowballing until it is so large it will steamroller me, probably when I am vulnerable and least expect it. By this time, the suffering I will have to bear will be considerable.

If I am eager to settle my accounts soon after they present themselves, a humble, aware attitude is vital. For example, a simple rule of thumb for settling accounts of negative karma is that I must give something that I have been unwilling to give. Living life in a way that embraces spiritual values, truth, humility and ethical conduct is the best way of avoiding negative karma, and it is the linchpin for settling karmic accounts. Of course, it is important to refrain from creating new accounts of impure action at the same time. Otherwise, I remain on the treadmill.

Living according to the highest moral and ethical principles forms the basis of a spiritual life. The Hindus recognise the spiritual principles specified in the *Bhagavad Gita*. These are primarily, *Brahmacharya*: meaning purity in thought, word and action, and includes celibacy; vegetarianism: as it is an act of violence to kill and eat the flesh which embodies a soul; following a pure diet: one that excludes alcohol, drugs, meat, eggs, onions and garlic; and *Ahimsa*: an ancient Jain commandment which involves non-violence towards all living things.

Becoming free of the vices of lust, anger, ego, greed and attachment is the aim in following a spiritual code of conduct. There is no better way to free your self from the effects of negative karma than living in accordance with these principles. To the average Westerner, these concepts may seem too difficult to contemplate, but they guarantee total freedom. Mohandas Gandhi followed them assiduously. The Brahma Kumaris also follow them. When embraced with true commitment and without compromise, these spiritual guidelines bring about profound transformation and arrest the accumulation of negative karmic accounts.

In general, some karmic accounts can be settled instantly, while other accounts may not rebound for many years or even lifetimes. For this reason, accounts within families can be very significant and intense. Within a lifetime, the soul will not settle all of its accounts. So unresolved accounts will carry over to the next life or lives, as the soul reincarnates. The natural laws are irrevocable, which means the soul is accountable for all of its actions. There is no immunity from the law of karma. These laws are not punitive, they are simply cause and effect. Whatever I do to or for another, I will experience myself in an exact and precise way. I also create accounts of karma regarding my own body. For instance, if I nourish, rest, exercise and look after my physical body well, it will give me the return of good health. If I eat junk food, drink too much and get insufficient exercise or rest, my body will eventually deliver the return on this too. Mentally, to work at maintaining a positive outlook and attitude means I develop a positive outlook and attitude. As the sixteenth-century proverb goes, virtue is its own reward.

Accounts of action are also experienced as imbalances or deficiencies through the personality. Redressing deficiencies means that whatever I lack, I first need to give. Restoring balance to the soul means literally that if I lack love in my life, then I must give it freely, without expectation of return. Mother Theresa spent much of her life caring for the dying Untouchables (the very poor people of India) in Calcutta. Service was her life's work and was clearly an expression of her innate tendencies and impressions. This was her way of expressing love and care to people alone, sick and dying on the street, in a city of profound deprivation.

Service plays an important role in spiritual development since it sets up an account of pure karma. Service is benevolent action that is given without any expectation of return, praise, payment or recognition. It is action donated or surrendered entirely to God, so it is pure action. Service is not just feeding the poor, helping the needy, reading to the blind or spending time with people who are sick and isolated; service can be carried out through mind, body, wealth and time in many ways. Service is never altruistic, because the principal beneficiary of service is always the self, and the good wishes and pure feelings that are returned to you have a very powerful effect.

By applying knowledge of the natural laws you can choose how you shape your future. Service is a dynamic key to this kind of transformation. While running groups for many years in a major correctional institution, I was once approached by a clerk who worked in the particular area I was connected with. Often I had observed how patient, loving and gentle his manner was when dealing with other inmates. He seemed exceptionally sincere, caring and tolerant in his dealings with everyone. In a prison setting his attitude stood out. During our conversation he explained that he had served a sentence of well over twenty years for murder and had been declared the most violent person in the maximum security prison where he was sent. In fact, he was so violent and out of control, the governor of the prison did not want him there at all but had to keep him. The authorities did not know what to do with him. As a consequence, it was decided he should spend four years in isolation. This, he said, gave him the opportunity to do a lot of soul-searching and thinking about himself. When the four years was up, he was put in touch with some people he described as extraordinarily kind and compassionate. He was so moved by their gentleness and caring, that he wrote down all of the things he loved and regarded so highly in the people who were helping him. Next, he wrote down all of the things he hated in himself. Finally, he made a decision to let go of all his negative traits and behaviours and take on the positive qualities of his helpers. I did not ask him about his religious beliefs, but his spirituality shone. From that time, his mission was to give to other inmates all that he had received. In this way, he had altered his fate dramatically. Thus by understanding the principle of 'action' it becomes clear to us how we can turn our fortunes around.

While the energy of karma is considered to be the most powerful force that governs us, there is one power that is greater — the Supreme Soul. The power of this Soul can finish negative traits and behaviours (like addictions) if we truly surrender them, in one second, forever. The more you deliver yourself from the burden of karma, the freer you become and the easier it is to connect with the Being of Light, because there is less interference from the personality. The more you link with this Soul in yoga, the more another very curious dynamic occurs. A kind of spiritual heat is created in this union, a heat that ignites the flame underneath the crucible. An intense fire of yoga burns away the impurity of the soul (which is the ego personality) and as this occurs, negative accounts of action are burned away and thus settled with it. This makes meditation a very powerful tool for self-transformation and for incinerating impure karma. In this way, freeing the self from the burden of karma is accomplished much more rapidly and effectively, than through suffering. It is understood that the fire of yoga will achieve a ninety-five per cent incineration of karma. The other five per cent will remain to be dealt with. It is essential to face all accounts of karma with humility, responsibility and a willingness to settle the account, to bring closure. If this means bowing to those who oppose you, then so be it.

The law of action is our greatest teacher, providing we develop the humility to accept what this teacher is telling us. Learning to accept, welcome and willingly settle our accounts is a passport to freedom, wisdom and super-sensuous joy. The freer the soul becomes, the more peaceful, blissful and radiant we become. A primary activity of the recently awakened soul is precisely this — settle, settle, settle. At the time of spiritual awakening and for some time afterwards, there tends to be an intensification of karmic settlement as the way is cleared for the soul to progress quickly.

Each of us has a karmic record which is imprinted and carried in the soul. It works like a bank account with a credit and debit column. When impure action is recorded you get an entry in the debit column, and when pure action is recorded you get an entry in the credit column. Meditation is pure action and a good way of 'injecting funds' into the account. Every time an account presents for settlement you will need sufficient 'funds' to deal with it. If the funds are lacking, what will happen? Uncomfortable feelings will arise and interest starts accruing. This continues until the debt is paid.

When a business fails and is bought out by another organi-sation, the organisation taking over makes an inventory of the debts and assets, settles the debts of the bankrupt company and assumes administrative leadership. It then carries on business, merging and effectively utilising the resources of the failed company. Karmically, when the soul engages in yoga with the Source the result is quite similar.

The course of self-change through Raja Yoga meditation runs thus: the first thing to change is attitude, the next thing is behaviour, third — innate tendencies or impressions in the soul change, fourth — your nature changes and finally, consciousness changes permanently. The very moment your attitude changes, your karma will begin to change. As the transformational process increases, your karma also changes progressively.

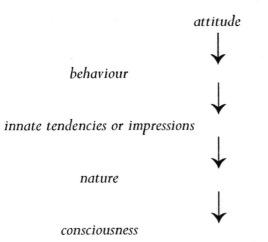

attitude

behaviour

innate tendencies or impressions

nature

consciousness

Diagram 4: *The process of change*

The natural laws not only govern individuals, they govern animals (which have souls), and also groups and nations. Heads of State, governments and religious leaders are not immune to the natural laws either, nobody is. The karma of protecting another person from the consequences of their own actions means you are taking on the karma of the person being protected. A wise and spiritually knowledgeable soul considers deeply the effects of their actions before acting.

Karma between nations is in the news constantly. In fact, nations have their own group karma, too. You can easily follow the account between the USA and the Middle East, the USA and Russia, India and Pakistan, Israel and Palestine. When the peace process fails and aggression escalates, the account between nations escalates. Engaging adversaries, making hostile demands and pursuing violent avenues serve to aggravate and increase accounts of action. The equalisation of karmic energy becomes an intense and unending drama. As greed, economic control, and racial or religious hatred fuel attitudes and conflict between nations and groups, the potential for devastation is incalculable.

It is easy to speak of a 'new world order', but who will bring it about? The only basis for a 'new world order' is spiritual change. Will politicians and economists really bring this change about? Will wars bring it about? Can human beings bring it about, or is intervention from a Higher Source the only way?

When human beings are soul-conscious there will be no violence and no peacelessness. To bring about a new world order, first we must change our consciousness. When the collective consciousness is free of the vices of lust, anger, ego, greed and attachment and the energy is raised to a high vibrational level, none of the current dilemmas in the world will exist. Until such time, the present world order of violence, suffering and greed will continue to be felt. This is the karma of our modern world.

chapter seven

HEALING ADDICTIONS

When the soul embarks on a path of spiritual growth, any blocks to growth in the personality will come to the fore sooner or later — this is the nature of the journey. If the blocks are side-stepped, spiritual growth will be arrested and we will find ourselves 'stuck'. But when the blocks are dealt with, energy bound up in those blockages is released and spiritual growth accelerates. Dealing positively with our ego-related blockages is what actually promotes our spiritual development. The most severe and destructive factor that the soul has to contend with presents as addictions and compulsions. In spiritual terms, the two worst things the soul can do to itself are commit suicide, and use drugs or succumb to other addictions. While the progress of an addiction may be slow or rapid, and the level of addiction be anywhere between mild or acutely life threatening; all addictions are progressive, and spiritually and psychologically damaging.

A curious dynamic exists between addiction and meditation which, simply put, is this — they do not support each other. In my case, within six to eight months of beginning to meditate, a number of my little habits had fallen away. If friends had not remarked on this I may never have noticed. Significantly, coffee and alcohol were next to go. Thus, within the first year I witnessed real change in myself, yet I was not consciously trying to change. Unfortunately, the road to spiritual perfection is not always like that. Some aspects of the self are transformed quite easily and quickly, while others refuse to budge.

With three years of meditation behind me and numerous attempts at quitting smoking, I had to accept that I was more addicted than ever to cigarettes, a reality that had come to sit rather uncomfortably with my conscience, fuelling a painful inner conflict. Smoking, it would seem, was my Achilles heel and was about to teach me a lesson. Spiritually, having a smoking habit was like trying to run with my ankles tied together, a fact that was constantly eroding my self-esteem. What I was not yet aware of was that dealing with my Achilles heel would offer me the most profound opportunity for growth imaginable.

For almost twenty years I had typically defended my habit with, 'I can quit whenever I want to', but now my moment of truth had come I was left feeling helpless and powerless. One day I opened the *LA Weekly*, which happened to be running a special on Twelve Step Programs, and staring straight at me was an article on Smokers Anonymous. My eyes seized on a paragraph, 'People who have quit all other drugs, including heroin, say that smoking is the most difficult addiction of all to quit.' I felt better already! 'Smokers find they have to keep going back to meetings because of the difficulty of staying stopped,' said the article, 'but despite these things many people do succeed in beating the habit permanently!' 'Great,' I thought, 'help at last!' I rang the telephone number at the bottom of the page and spoke to a woman who listened empathically, reassuring me that she had quit successfully six years ago. 'Can you meet me at the Beverly Hills meeting on Monday night?' she asked. 'I'll be there!' I answered.

We met at the entrance to a large hall where a couple of hundred chairs were set out. I took a seat at the back as the hall filled up, and listened with interest to the stories people were sharing about their countless attempts to quit, how they would end up slinking off to the 7-Eleven at two or three in the morning for their drug, and the mounting years of denial about their addiction. I related to every single thing I heard, it was as if they were talking about me! But internally a part of me was resisting. At the end of the meeting, people stood up one by one and identified themselves by their first name, followed by 'I'm a nicotine addict.' I decided that I most definitely would not do that! Yet when it came to my turn I seemed to be on my feet gushing embarrassingly about how hopeless I felt and how I really needed help. Hearing myself say these things brought extraordinary relief. Afterwards, people approached me and said they could relate to where I was at because they had been there. I was offered much encouragement and reassurance.

I pored over the literature tables and came away with a huge pile of reading material, covering everything from the Twelve Steps to tips on quitting and graphic articles on lung disease, cancer and emphysema. Before the next meeting I had smoked my final cigarette! With the assistance of the reading material I brainwashed myself with statistics, medical articles and horror stories about smokers inhaling cigarettes through tracheotomies until they died of emphysema. This kept my mind engaged in a positive way as I had a great need to distract myself from any thoughts about smoking. Thinking about smoking a cigarette had brought me undone every single time I had tried to quit. This time I was determined!

Despite severe gut pain, dizziness, disorientation in the world, and other withdrawal symptoms, I began to get the feeling I would make it. My resolve, which had been fuzzy in the past, was firming up. Cravings that would almost render me insensible came in waves, but I learned at the meetings that I could say 'no' to cravings, they were not my master. As time passed the cravings were less frequent and eventually, less intense. At times I chewed nicotine gum, but I was not prepared to pick up that first cigarette — and the compulsion to smoke left me. The miracle came at last and my resolve turned to steel. Hollywood was very much a smoking town in those days, before the purist movement purged LA of smoky workplaces. This meant I was surrounded by cigarettes, smoke and ashtrays at work, in fact almost everywhere I went except the meditation centre. People were constantly lighting up and blowing smoke in my face, leaving lit cigarettes burning in ashtrays under my nose, or wandering off leaving packets of cigarettes and lighters at my disposal. A mantra emerged from my lips at least a hundred times a day, 'I don't do that any more.'

Often, I had ruminated on the idea that if ever I could be free of my physical addictions, that would be it — end of story. I could never see beyond those things. However, once I was free of the gross dependencies I realised this was only the beginning. Next came the daunting, if not devastating realisation that I had to deal with *me* now. All my underlying patterns and behaviours, like a veritable Pandora's Box, lay waiting — I just knew it! From the depth of my being came an agonised groan. Without a smoke-screen to hide behind the truth was finally, unavoidably in my face: clean out the entire closet or there will always be a reason to pick up a cigarette — or something else!

I began to understand very clearly why people relapse with addictions, and how true commitment to self-change is the only way to freedom. If there was an easy way out of addiction no one had found it yet. Sitting through meetings I learned a great deal about pain and failure, rejection and abandonment, compassion, empathy and truth. I learned to be open about myself, to hear myself expose parts of me that were secret; to be breathtakingly honest about aspects of me that made me feel ashamed; and I experienced the healing, acceptance and liberation this brings. I felt much in those meetings because I was constantly touched by the experiences of others. Now, relative to the *satsang*, it seemed I was really in the 'company of truth'. I began to develop a deep love and respect for the uncompromising honesty that flowed through these gatherings. This level of honesty was possible because of the anonymity, acceptance and lack of judgement. Bonds of empathy and love grew with friends I made in the meetings, as something hurt and aching inside me was being honoured and nurtured into healing.

Most of all, I began to experience a much closer and more intimate relationship with the Soul who was always subtly guiding, prompting, humouring and encouraging me. With the guidance of my program 'sponsor' and by opening up to all that was weak, shameful and defective in my character, I was developing a much more mature and meaningful relationship with God. As a meditator, the recovery journey enabled me to develop valuable insights into the spiritual process of addiction. The power of meditation was nourishing my healing and progress. Many people from the meetings could see it and were curious about what I was doing.

Each one of the twelve steps in the recovery program involves a spiritual undertaking which has a direct impact on our karma. Working through these steps engenders humility and reduces the karmic burden of the past. The steps also reinforce spiritual values and an ethical code of conduct, instilling morality and scrupulous honesty as a means of redressing degradation of character. With the power of meditation, there is probably no more effective tool for accelerated spiritual growth than the Twelve Steps.

Finding a cure for addictions is an age-old pursuit and one which has not enjoyed riveting success. Freud became addicted to cocaine while experimenting with the drug on himself in the hope of finding a cure for his friend who was addicted to heroin. Not only was he unable to help his friend, he was unable to help himself and was in the grip of cocaine addiction until his death. Carl Jung had great insight into addiction and also struggled with his own compulsions. He believed that a spiritual awakening was the key to healing addiction.

But just what is addiction? The World Health Organisation once defined it as 'a pathological relationship to any mood or mind-altering substance, person, place, event, experience or thing which has life-damaging consequences.' The two things that hold addictions in place are denial and rationalisation, and herein the vicious cycle of addiction becomes entrenched.

Many addictions such as over-achieving and chronic over-working are socially sanctioned (and even encouraged in the workplace) compared to dependencies on substances, but they rob the soul of spiritual power and destroy the balance and quality of life, just as chemical dependency does. For the soul to progress spiritually, all addictions, no matter how acceptable or subtle, must be addressed.

Whatever age a person is when they begin 'using', is the age they will remain emotionally. Once chemical dependency or other forms of addiction are adopted, the emotional maturing process is halted. Since the human brain does not complete it's development until the age of about twenty-eight, introducing highly toxic substances like alcohol and drugs into the system regularly, in earlier years, can do significant damage.

The presence of addiction represents our psychological 'governing system', which means that the addiction controls our decision-making, choices, behaviour, interactions and life. Because addiction is a progressive disease, it will not magically disappear, it inevitably gets worse over time. Until appropriate intervention is sought and put into practice, nothing will change.

There are three main stages of recovery. The first stage is called Recovery, and refers to detoxification, or physical and mental withdrawal. When withdrawals are finished and a stable abstinence program is established, which takes about twelve months, the Uncovery stage begins. This involves uncovering and working through all of the underlying reasons for using or acting-out. Working a recovery program and engaging in regular counselling or psychotherapy sessions are important for facilitating Uncovery work. The third stage (which can be initiated as soon as withdrawals are over) is referred to as Discovery, meaning discovery of the spiritual self, leading to a spiritual awakening. Meditation facilitates this level of recovery specifically, and is a very powerful avenue for healing, particularly in conjunction with the Twelve Steps. A spiritual awakening is considered to be a vital aspect of the recovery journey. Those who have walked the path understand the level of commitment and determination that are necessary for a full recovery and the freedom this brings.

There is no quick or easy way to deal with addictions. Substitute pills, drugs or other activities do not replace the hard work on the self that is required to recover. Even in established recovery, the temptation to use substitutions may be present. Substitutions can involve seemingly harmless activities like watching too much television; excessive shopping and spending; or over-indulgence in food, sex or exercise, to get the 'high' or feeling of 'being fixed'.

The fact is, that underneath all addictions lies a vast empty pit. Avoiding that pit may have been our life's work so far, but in recovery the pit has to be faced. Addictions are a way of filling the pit, or void, so as not to be pulled in to it. The paradox is, that only by going into the very depth of the void can we find our true selves and heal. The ego mightily resists doing this, whereas the soul supports it completely. Meditation and a spiritual opening-up play an important role in healing at this level.

Effect of the 'Using Repertoire' on the Soul

Any addiction or compulsive behaviour causes impairment of spiritual function. Obsessive–compulsive patterns of feeling, thinking and acting leave deep impressions in the memory. With prolonged repetition, the deeply scoured habit impressions result in automatic behaviour. In the early stages of an addiction the intellect and conscience speak with a clear voice, but when this voice is acted against or ignored time and time again, it cuts out. It is as though the metaphysical 'nerve' which connects the mind with the intellect and conscience is severed (see Diagram 5). This disconnection destroys spiritual and moral integrity in the person as impulses triggered by the habit act directly on the will. The mind and inner function of a chronically addicted person becomes completely overtaken by impulses from the person's 'using repertoire'. A 'using repertoire' may consist of three stages: 'get the money, get the drugs, get on'. This repertoire digs the person ever more deeply into a hole, as normal life activities are increasingly relinquished for the drug of choice. Without any higher function, the person is simply driven by impulse.

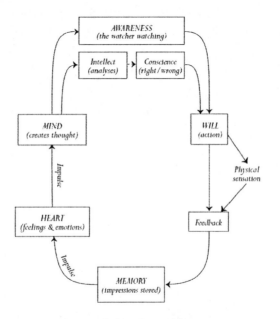

Diagram 5: Normal spiritual function

Each thought passes from the mind through the intellect and conscience, before being expressed or acted upon by the will. In this way our spiritual faculties or 'organs' ensure that our words, expressions and actions, are in accord with our spiritual integrity.

Negative emotions which drive the addiction cycle, link with the impulse from the memory as well, and become deeply and powerfully reinforced in the memory. Awareness, which is informed by every aspect of inner function, becomes blocked, blinded, and ceases to work. This means the person is unaware of

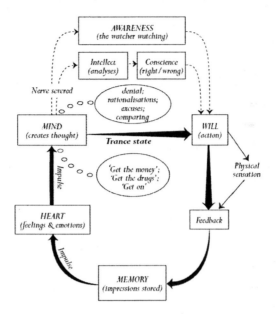

Diagram 6: *Obsessive–compulsive pattern of addiction*

Instead of thoughts from the mind going to the intellect then conscience, before acting on
the will, the person puts him-her self into a trance state and the impulse from the
impression goes directly from the mind to the will, where it is acted out, unmediated.
Impulsive and compulsive action results when the 'nerve' connecting the mind and
intellect is severed. The person will say, 'I did it without thinking!'

what they are doing to themselves, or the effect they are having on those who love and care about them. Addiction is the strongest way the soul disconnects from itself.

The using repertoire narrows and constricts a person's inner and outer world to such a degree that insight completely disappears. Intellect and conscience are like navigation equipment, our rudder and compass, directing and guiding us through daily life. Combined with awareness they facilitate insight and are involved in every aspect of decision making. Each thought the mind creates passes through the intellect and conscience under normal circumstances. When the intellect and conscience are bypassed, all insight, sense of direction and inner guidance disappear and awareness is blocked, until eventually the feeling of being lost is overwhelming. The addicted person experiences being so deeply dug-in, that they can no longer see beyond their own inner turmoil. They cannot see a way out. When the drug has ceased to have a strong effect, a consequence of prolonged and heavy usage, the dependant no longer has the drug's 'high' to mask their pain and chaos. They must face their moral degradation and feel fully, the sense of inner, spiritual collapse.

The person who uses until they hit rock bottom experiences only pain and insanity. Drugs, alcohol, gambling, work, sex, food, in fact any addiction at all, is a massive analgesic to begin with. When the analgesia stops working and the person is faced with whatever issues they are medicating, plus the consequences of the turmoil and chaos their life has usually descended into, they require appropriate support, counselling and guidance to face up to things squarely and get back on track. When there is damage to the soul's functioning, meditation can facilitate a spiritual healing process.

As soon as a person begins meditating they begin to experience a sense of peace. The factor which drives addiction is experienced as a spiral into negative emotion, and sometimes termed 'spiritual bankruptcy', is directly addressed through twelve step action and meditation. Empowering the soul promotes healing at physical, mental and emotional levels of being, as well as at the spiritual level. Elevated anxiety levels usually precede the desire to use a drug or activity of addiction, and this is a major factor in relapse. Meditation can reduce anxiety significantly. The more dedicated and committed the person is to meditating, the more healing and benefit they experience.

The stereotype of a down-and-out, unwashed junkie or alcoholic convinces many people with serious addictions that they 'aren't that bad', or that they 'don't really have a problem'. The vast majority of people with addictions, including alcoholics and addicts, hold down responsible jobs, dress well, have families and look perfectly 'normal'. This is where denial and rationalisation come in. Lying, deceit, manipulation, leading a double-life and indulging in complex games, are behaviours common to any addiction. Family members also fall victim to the addiction, as they learn to collude with the dependent's dysfunctional behaviour by supporting their lies, caretaking them, and protecting them from the consequences of their behaviour. This collusion is commonly known as 'enabling'.

It is vital that the dependent person's lies, behaviour, denial, rationalisation and using are openly challenged, and this is precisely what occurs in Twelve Step programs and appropriate counselling. Dependent people may also invent a litany of excuses for rejecting Twelve Step and other recovery programs. For example, among many I have heard: 'I can't go to AA because I'm a doctor/counsellor/actor' to 'I don't like the people at the meetings, they've all got serious problems', or 'I don't like the meetings because I only like being around nice, white, middle-class, educated people.' Families, friends and even helping professionals who do not know any better will collude with the excuses and continue 'enabling' the dependent person to practise their addiction. A person who has been raised with addiction in the family will be well trained in the art of 'enabling'. Davey's story illustrates this.

Davey was a lovely little toddler of two and a half when his father, a self-employed house painter, developed an exacerbated problem with binge drinking. Most of the time his father worked very hard, but now he began staying out all night and was too hungover and sick to go to work when he was drinking. This pattern gradually increased as Davey grew. By the time Davey started school, he was used to hearing his mother on the phone apologising to customers and lying about malaria and tropical diseases. His mother would say 'Daddy's sick today,' yet the drinking was never mentioned. As

Davey grew older he accepted the lies, as he had been trained to do, although he knew perfectly well what the stench of alcohol and the behaviour that went with it meant. The convention of lies around his father's alcoholism was well established and developed more and more as the drinking increased. As an adult he realised the words 'alcoholic' and 'drunk' were taboo in the household and never mentioned. So were his father's drink-driving charges, visits by police, or the financial shortages that he knew caused his mother much anxiety and pain, despite her keeping up a brave front and managing the money with great care. Deprived of close bonding and a real relationship with his father, Davey grew up with a deep father-hunger. His mother's constant distraction with worry and anger meant she was never emotionally available for her son, thus in a sense Davey lost both his parents.

How can a child hold on to his spiritual integrity when family and societal messages continually confuse, contradict and erode it? Children like Davey become high risk. At least half of them will be looking for a way of filling their own emptiness with food, substances or problem behaviours by the end of primary school, or later on will find an alcoholic/addict to partner with — like a homing pigeon.

Meditation is certainly not a panacea for addiction, but it does address spiritual healing and supports healing at the other levels. A wholistic approach is the best insurance against relapse or incomplete recovery.

During a study conducted in the early 1990s in Sydney, where people in rehabilitation centres were taught to meditate as soon as they had detoxified and were thereafter supported with their meditation for periods of up to six months and longer, some important changes were noted. Primary among these was a significantly increased level of motivation, interest in and energy for recovery compared with the groups who were not meditating. The people in the groups who were meditating experienced a drop in anxiety levels and reported a sense of inner calm and peace. They also reported receiving a natural feeling of intoxication from their meditation experiences, which they felt replaced the high of chemicals in a very fulfilling way.[12] Restoring balance is a principal factor in early, medium and long-term recovery, which is why a well thought out wholistic approach provides the best possible support for those who are ready and willing to change.

While I was in Vietnam during 2000, training psychiatrists and social workers who were working with heroin addicts, I became acquainted with a very different approach. During the training, questions arose several times around the issue of clients wanting to leave the centre to go away and continue their heroin use. Each time I answered this question the same way, saying that no one can be forced into recovery. Recovery is a voluntary act and when a person is ready he or she will reach out for help. I also explained that addicts may go through 'detox' and 'rehab' numerous times before they are ready to take the final step and embrace a drug-free lifestyle. Any movement towards detoxification or recovery should be seen as a positive step in what may be a long, cumulative process for many addicts, and any positive movement is deserving of support. But it seemed that most of the psychiatrists did not understand what I was saying. Finally, on the last day of training the question arose again, framed in terms of, 'How can we make them want recovery, when they want to use drugs?' This time I asked questions about how they assessed their clients. What was revealed came as a shock. Addicts, they told me, were usually picked up from the street (although it is not illegal to use heroin in Vietnam) and put into an institution under lock and key for a forced detox and rehabilitation program. The latter consisted of 'education', which was principally focused on studying Stalin's political doctrine and was not remotely connected with anything that would help them recover. Naturally, they wanted to escape and would often try to, so high perimeter fences and armed guards were employed to prevent this from happening. 'What happens after they've detoxed?' I asked. 'Many commit suicide,' was the reply.

Being a drug addict brings with it a stigma and loss of social status in any society. The Asian addict, in particular, struggles with a strong cultural issue in recovery — the shame and dishonour they bring upon their family. As all nations attempt to grapple with policing, trafficking, dealing, police corruption, crime, overdose deaths, harm minimisation and addiction; it is important that the person who really needs and wants help to recover does not get overlooked in the wider system.

In summary, by understanding the spiritual, psychological and physical dimensions of addiction, we are better equipped to deal with it in an enlightened way and to use our helping resources wisely and compassionately. We know that effective intervention in the cycle of addiction comes about by addressing the condition of spiritual bankruptcy that drives all addiction. Addressing spiritual bankruptcy changes the governing system of addiction. Recovery, Uncovery and Discovery are the three stages of healing addiction, from the initial physical and mental withdrawals, to the work of uncovering the underlying reasons for using, and nourishing the path of spiritual awakening. It is vital to address the 'using repertoire' and resulting disconnection between the mind and conscience, with meditation and a recovery program. Finally, addressing the spiritual void is essential to a full recovery from addiction. Healing addiction does not involve 'cure', thus sobriety or abstinence, one day at a time, is fundamental to ongoing healing and spiritual growth.

Contrary to impressions created by the media, many heroin and other drug addicts do recover fully, creating very worthwhile lives and helping many others like themselves. Service, giving back what has been received and supporting others, creates a great mantle of growth, protection and community in the world of shared healing and recovery.

During the 1980s the United Nations World Health Organisation labelled addiction 'the crisis of our time'. Over the past few decades the crisis of addiction stands out in social history and is here to teach us something important about ourselves, our civilisation and where we are heading, if only we can develop the willingness to look inwards.

Addictions and compulsions are not the only thing that hold the soul to ransom. Another curious dynamic exists very commonly in our society but passes seemingly without notice or mention. While working with people in recovery from substance abuse, this secondary issue became evident to me. It is an issue that not only plays a pivotal role in addiction, but for many becomes an unacknowledged part of everyday life. I call it suffering from a spiritual allergy. Our spiritual allergies litter the pathway to higher consciousness.

chapter eight

SPIRITUAL ALLERGIES

Carrie bolted into my office and put her bag down. Throwing her arms into the air above her head she said, 'I don't believe it! He's deserted me!'

'Not your husband?' I exclaimed, surprised.

'No, my Higher Power! Just because I stopped following the program, just because I stopped doing what HE wanted! And I'm angry!' Carrie was in the Overeaters Anonymous Program and had endured a long-term struggle to achieve abstinence, when she decided to try some counselling. She had just begun to experience her first taste of abstinence — for a blissful three weeks. 'He left me, just like that!' she repeated grimly, looking angrily in my direction.

I asked her to speak to her Higher Power, and using an empty chair, I suggested she 'put' her Higher Power on the chair and address her Higher Power directly. She shrugged as though to say, what good will that do? Then she began, 'The moment I stop doing what you want, you can't be bothered with me! I've been trying so hard and as soon as I slip that's it, you dump me!'

'And you remind me of ...' I chimed in, touching her lightly on the shoulder.

'You're just like my father! My whole childhood was like this.' Carrie stopped in her tracks and fell silent. 'I had no idea that was going to come out,' she said, shocked. 'I've been feeling so much resentment towards him, I mean my Higher Power. Now I can see the issue is really with my father, that is what he was like! I worked so hard to become the person he wanted me to be, to do what he wanted, so that he would love me. But the moment I did something he disapproved of, that was it, he cut me off.' She fell silent.

How was Carrie going to trust again? She had been attending OA on and off for two years but was unable to 'get it'. As long as the image of her father who abandoned her was being subconsciously projected onto her Higher Power, abstinence was an elusive dream and Carrie was caught up in a cycle of rejecting her recovery group. This is all it takes to contaminate a person's relationship with a Higher Power. Until the original rupture with the parent is brought fully into awareness and the unfinished business resolved, therapeutically at least, the projection of the pain and the deficit in trust will continue subconsciously to undermine attempts to recover or to forge a trusting relationship with another. It is not only the Higher Power who receives the 'bad father' projection, but is also most likely to be the intimate partner and the person in the helping role (among others). Discerning and uncovering what I term 'spiritual allergies' is pivotal to spiritual growth and recovery.

My introduction to work in the field of chemical dependency brought me face to face with a group of people I loved being with, who, in the short and the long term, brought me much closer to myself. They identified themselves as having addictions to drugs and alcohol, and some of them acknowledged they were drug dealers, prostitutes or criminals. Initially, the doorbell would ring day and night at the meditation centre in an inner city suburb of Sydney (which has since closed), and when I answered the door, it was often someone drug or alcohol affected asking for help. I was there to use the computer and I was not sure what to say. One afternoon I walked into the lobby to witness a transsexual wearing fishnet stockings and very high heels being attended by an awkward, though caring, meditation instructor. He stiffly offered the transsexual (who was quite beside himself, looking dishevelled, distraught and extremely drug-affected) a couple of aspirin and a glass of water, as the fellow's mascara ran down his face forming large, black rivers of tears. Somehow, the sight of this man's encounter with the scrubbed, squeaky-clean, homophobic, utterly stricken meditator in his perfectly starched and ironed whites, so moved me with compassion, I later suggested we do something for people who came to the door asking for help. As I have learned over many years in a voluntary organisation, suggestions like these are how I get myself a job. 'That's a good idea Judi. You do it!' he replied.

After that, anyone who rang the doorbell asking for help and was willing to come back when they were not drug-affected, was offered a course in meditation. I taught them in small and large groups. They would talk to me about their drug issues, their recovery problems, their relationships and marriages, their child-hoods, religious training, 'rehab', gaol, their parents and their families. Within all this, I was learning much about what I was then just beginning to understand to be spiritual allergies. A spiritual allergy is caused by a conscious or subconscious feeling of disappointment, resistance, fear, betrayal, hurt, anger or bitterness towards a primary caregiver, religious representative or authority figure, which is unconsciously transferred onto a Higher Source. Forming and engaging in a trusting connection with that Source, under these circumstances, poses a major hurdle.

With few exceptions, it was obvious that these people used substances to survive conscious and subconscious memories of neglect, violation and trauma. In the process of becoming addicted, it seemed they had come to worship a false god, one who would guarantee a predictable but temporary 'high' at a price. Spiritual allergies were in abundance, and identifying and deconstructing them became an important part of our work at the centre.

Spiritual allergies are easy to catch. The generalised tendency to blame God for our own negative accounts of karma, or to hold God responsible for every painful occurrence in life, is one contributing factor. The following example is from the memoirs of writer Alexandre Dumas.[13] He recalls the tragic loss of his father when he was four years of age. In the aftermath of his father's death, Alexandre wanted to know who had killed his father and where he was. After being informed by a relative that it was God's will that his father had died and that his father was now in heaven with God, the devastated young child was so enraged that he found his father's gun and went upstairs to get closer to heaven, with the idea that he would kill God for the crime of taking his father. At age four Alexandre's trust and belief in a protecting and loving God was painfully shattered.

Natural calamities, the death of loved ones and other disturbing events over which we have no control are not acts of divine retribution, as many people assume. But this is the kind of thinking that can subtly influence our attitude towards a Higher Being.

Abusive behaviour by officers of the church clearly represents a proportion of spiritual allergies, but the deliberate promotion of guilt and a 'God-fearing' culture in religion also plays a significant role in causing a person's relationship with the Source to become distorted and ruptured. It is impossible to reconcile such a God with the loving, compassionate, accepting and non-judgemental instrument portrayed by Christ. Childhood is a time of extreme vulnerability to spiritual allergies. Many people have shared stories with me that marked the beginning of such an experience.

A seven-year-old girl is told a story by her teacher at Sunday School about a little Protestant girl who does not believe that the wine and bread given at the Catholic mass or Holy Communion are really the flesh and blood of Christ. The story tells how the Protestant girl gets her little Catholic friend who does believe, to take the bread home and stick a needle in it. The Catholic girl agrees, takes her communion bread home and goes to the kitchen, whereupon she sticks a needle into the bread. Blood flows from the bread, the story goes, until it fills the whole kitchen.

The seven-year old wonders why such an extraordinary event, if it is true, was not in the papers. Shortly afterwards the same child announces to her mother that she will not go back to Sunday School again. Why? Because she does not believe the story about the blood filling the kitchen and she is fed up with inventing 'sins' to tell the priest at confession.

◊

A woman finds the familiar patriarchal image of God as an old man with a beard, a punishing God, so like her own father — a hostile and abusive man — that she wants nothing to do with God. She does not even want to think about God because the memory of her father is too painful.

◊

A young man weeps as he breaks his silence for the first time and recalls being molested and raped by a school master as a young boy at a church-run boarding school, a situation which continued for several years. He painfully remembers the shame, the inability to tell anyone including his parents, and how eventually he tried to kill himself in the school grounds. The same school master assaulted several other boys, one of whom took him to court on charges of paedophilia, but lost the case. He believes the church failed to protect him as a schoolboy and that even now it protects the man who perpetrated the crimes. Adding to his suffering is the fact that his relationship with his father is emotionally distant. He hungers for his father's love and support, for a close bond that is denied him. Spiritually he feels deserted and alone.

◊

A woman recalls how she was raped by her father from the age of three to fifteen, on a daily basis. He ranted and raved about Christ and the Bible, about sin and morality, how she was evil, dirty and tainted and had been sent by the devil to tempt him. Well before she began kindergarten, her father had convinced her she was responsible for what he was doing. Eventually, he drove himself mad and was taken away. Although she has not been near a church since marrying at eighteen to get away from home, she has been able to find a healing relationship with a God of her own understanding, that excludes the church and focuses on her own inner experience of this Soul.

There are so many stories like these. How often has someone asked the question, 'Why didn't God protect me?' or, 'If God really loved me how could He let that happen?' Not surprisingly, these are the questions children and adults ask. Sadly, our Western theology and philosophy has no response except perhaps the rather unhelpful (as was told to Alexandre Dumas) 'It was God's will'. Spiritual allergies can result when we feel betrayed or abandoned by God, or if there is a wounding in the soul's relationship with a Higher Being. The wounds may not be something we are consciously aware of, however.

In contrast to the Western approach, Hindus exhibit a much more joyful attitude towards religion. The Hindu religions celebrate their many deities and occasions of religious significance with one religious festival after another, all year round. They dress up, do puja or religious rituals and worship, play devotional music, beat drums, cook special food, dance and enjoy themselves, sometimes for days and nights on end. This is their culture. They also honour the birth of all the religious founders.

For the person from a Christian culture who has arrived at their moment of reckoning, perhaps through an addiction, life crisis or life-threatening illness, the question of spiritual allergy may be very much in the foreground, although not consciously. It is because faith is called into question that such an obstacle arises. The nature of an individual's relationship with their parents may well impact on that person's ability to relate to and trust God as a father or mother. God is referred to as 'the Father' by most religious traditions, so most people will naturally project some aspects of their personal father or mother onto God consciously or unconsciously. If the father relationship is complete and fulfilled this will probably enhance the quality of a relationship with God, but if it is incomplete it may well detract from this relationship. Similarly, when a person's relationship with their mother is blocked or troubled, the effect on the relationship with God may well reflect a similar deficit.

People in recovery from addictions wishing to form a relationship with a Higher Power have to face the issue of 'surrender' sooner or later, handing 'their will and their life over to the care of the God of their understanding.'[14] This process of surrendering tends to bring out spiritual allergies dramatically and is clearly designed for this very purpose. The word 'surrender' can have deep and difficult implications for many a soul where power has been abused, even quite subtly, in childhood and, of course, later in life. While millions of people surrender to drugs, destructive relationships and other addictions without a qualm, facing the kind of surrender that recovery requires may be intensely confronting.

Childhood influences are extremely powerful and create a lasting impression on the personality. For many people, finding a trusting relationship with a Higher Power is vital to their healing process, whether it is physical, psychological or spiritual. Past experiences involving betrayal of trust, abuse, abandonment and non-valuing of the person, inevitably create blocks. When a child's power is violated, repercussions in the adult are very serious. Spiritual allergies need to be examined carefully and brought into awareness, as they can interfere with spiritual development in subtle yet damaging ways.

The woman who has learned such mistrust of men that she secretly even fears her own husband and sons, and who is struggling to develop a healing relationship with God, could have a wide chasm to negotiate. This applies just as much to men who have suffered at the hands of male or female authority figures. Many children have a natural, unspoken relationship with a loving, nurturing God. It is in their consciousness well before birth and as they grow it is either reinforced or damaged. It is one thing when this special relationship is not supported by caregivers, but when a child's relationship with God is deliberately violated by caregivers who have evil intent, this is entirely another issue. The karma attached to such action is extremely severe. Every child has a right to have their own special inner relationship with an unconditionally loving God and to know this God will love and support them no matter what, just as they are. This is unrelated to any religious belief system, it is more a basic human spiritual right. To deprive a child of this right is deeply wounding.

Spiritual allergies usually begin in childhood and are cultivated from then on. It is reported in the media how many of the younger generations have a deep sense of despair and hopelessness about the future of humanity, resulting in lack of motivation, depression and the absence of inspiration or purpose. The human spirit wilts without value, love and recognition. Life without a spiritual purpose is meaningless for many adults and so, it seems, for children. Without spiritual truth, knowledge and values; hope and optimism founder.

Hindus I have met or observed in the East seem to suffer very little with spiritual allergies, possibly because their deities are protective and benevolent. Of course, atheism and agnosticism do exist, especially among the educated middle classes of India.

Religion is so interwoven with the fabric of existence in India, it cannot be separated. If you wander through the Ajmal Khan

Park in Karol Bagh, Delhi, you will hear the sounds of chanting and see smoky clouds of strongly aromatic incense rising in the predawn darkness. Men sit on little prayer rugs or on the cold ground, performing *puja* (religious ritual, worship) as the grey light of morning filters through the heavy haze of pollution that hangs over Delhi.

Early evening *satsangs* or spiritual gatherings take place in Ajmal Khan. The little park has a community of outdoor residents, all of whom stake their claim for a piece of ground. It is the only home many of these people know. The very poor rickshaw wallahs who ride bicycles, live along one side of the park fence, next to an open sewerage drain. They sleep side by side and eat, cook, wash and do their laundry together every day, hanging their washing over the park fence to dry each morning. Then they go to work. For many souls living in abject poverty, religion is the mainstay and meaning of their existence, they have nothing else. Despite their poverty and deprivation, supported by their faith in their gods, they always seem to have a warm smile and appear much happier than the well-heeled tourist from the West. They do not know the pressures and stresses of Western materialism and in this sense they are blissfully free.

Common to both East and West is a particular type of arrogance connected with the ego identity of being a 'spiritual person'. This kind of arrogance manifests in phoney humility and the desire to have others believe that either they are God or more elevated than everyone else. When spiritual teachers suffer from spiritual arrogance, they are not able to bring others closer to God because they seek followers and devotees for themselves. When a 'teacher' has made considerable spiritual effort and is able to articulate spiritual knowledge well and move people, he or she needs to be very pure of heart and attitude not to fall into the invisible trap of spiritual ego.

A true teacher does not place him- or herself 'above' anyone, look down on anyone, or tolerate let alone encourage 'devoteeism'. The guru fantasy is a grand illusion constructed by the personality, whereby a human being is attributed Godlike qualities, status and powers. The guru fantasy occurs in the religious and spiritual movements, supported by those who want to 'follow' a human being. When cults, sects and religions fall apart, the disillusioned, who may have placed their wealth and faith in the hands of a human leader, may need a great deal of debriefing. To abandon basic integrity when on a devotional path is to invite trouble. Bad experiences like these set up powerful spiritual allergies. The discriminating spiritual seeker, however, will not find spiritual arrogance attractive and will most likely be repelled by it.

Spiritual allergies are important indicators, alerting us to be wary of pretenders, hypocrites and people who are only serving their self-interest no matter in whose name they claim authority. They sharpen our discrimination and teach us to trust our intuitive feelings about teachings, philosophies, and spiritual and religious paths. These matters involve deeply personal choices and are not necessarily anyone else's business. When the teacher, practice or teaching is not congruent with spiritual values, our inner alarm bells should be sounding loudly. Congruence is the key when checking out a spiritual practice. For example, the spiritual teacher who smokes, drinks or behaves in spiritually incongruous ways; the articulate spiritual leader who runs a wealthy organisation, owns a stable of status cars, whose programs are always jammed with celebrities; or the teacher who exhibits a penchant for media hype and star status are not spiritually accurate.

The wary, discriminating, even cynical soul will be attracted to that which has about it a feeling of sincerity, truth and simplicity. The Dalai Lama's humility, natural warmth, compassion and simplicity attract many people, regardless of whether or not they are Buddhists. His authenticity and deep wisdom appeal to people of many faiths, and so he stands out from the crowd of contemporary sages and spiritual leaders.

Spiritual allergies are a reaction to religious and spiritual people, and to teachings and practices that are hypocritical, wounding and devaluing of the beauty of the human spirit. They are a reaction to that which pretends to be religious or spiritual, or which masquerades as God. Spiritual allergies, with their accompanying feeling of irritation, let us know when a so-called religious or spiritual environment is not for us. Allergies of this nature need to be understood, for they can also awaken us through irritation, sending us on our quest.

Out of the blue, the soul can be touched by the gentleness of God — then spiritual love awakens a deep feeling of trust. When the one true love is found, silence and peace fill our hearts once more.

chapter nine

'DYING ALIVE'

Developing the willingness to deal with addictions and spiritual allergies enables the soul to move forwards by great leaps, despite often feeling as though the opposite is occurring. A curious dynamic in the healing process is one we call 'dying alive'. It facilitates letting go and is really a death of part of the ego. Because the ego's movement is towards resistance and holding on; conflict, tension, anxiety and pain are inevitable precursors to letting go, in the act of 'dying alive'. When we 'die alive' we willingly sacrifice ego in service of our spiritual growth.

When the soul leaves the body during the transition we call dying, it undergoes an experience in which attachment to things, situations, loved ones and to the various roles we have created and played out in life, and even to our own body image, are (ideally) let go. During this process, the layers of ego that have accumulated around the soul dissolve, so that the soul is completely revealed in its essential, egoless state. To be with a dying person in what Elizabeth Kübler-Ross[15] refers to as their 'stage of acceptance', is to experience the energy and beauty of the soul in a state of serene, loving detachment. The process of 'dying alive' which is associated with the journey to spiritual completion is similar, except that it occurs without actual separation of the soul and the physical body.

Just as a dying person who reaches the stage of acceptance makes peace with themselves and others; experiencing liberation from all of the needs, desires and attractions associated with their body and physical relationships; so the soul on the spiritual

95

path can achieve the same freedom during life. 'Dying alive' means learning to detach from the physical, sensual and emotional drives in an easy, peaceful and loving manner. Quite distinct from repressing our drives, the result of 'dying alive' is self-mastery, complete freedom and transcendence into the super-sensuous experience of the spirit. Just as the dying person's acceptance brings them into a very pure, serene and loving state of detachment, similarly, 'dying alive' brings the soul into the same easy, loving detachment and mastery over the body. Moving beyond all struggle, the soul is released from its enslavement to the physical, sensual and emotional drives, and once more takes its rightful place as a sovereign being. The body then truly becomes the 'temple of the soul', rather than its prison or battlefield. Instead of the soul leaving the body, it simply leaves its old consciousness.

Naturally, power and spiritual knowledge are required to undergo this death of the personality or ego. At the slightest threat to its existence, the automatic movement of the ego is to hold on. Because ego is society-driven and validated, and because society is largely ego-driven and the ruling power, the achievement of ego death is of great significance. Spiritual growth often involves a strong element of going against the accepted social norm — of doing something that society (in curious and subtle ways) marginalises, fears and devalues.

Ego-consciousness brings us into powerful emotional states which can be experienced at full force. Such states include anger, jealousy, resentment, bitterness, anxiety, panic, fear, hate, desire, attachment, dependency and neediness, to mention but a few. Emotions are reactions to people or events, which are generated within the personality. Energy drives emotions and even more energy is bound up in repressing them. Emotional reactivity is a double-edged sword because on the one hand we are taught it is good to let our emotions out and express ourselves, yet on the other, we may face censorship and alienation when we do so.

Learning to express our emotions appropriately and effectively is part of the maturing process called differentiation, which is intricately linked to spiritual growth. It means being able to separate our feelings from our thinking. A person with a high level of maturity is informed by and is in good contact with their emotions, yet is able to express themselves and act appropriately, using both their emotions and their intellect separately and with great discernment. They are also able to 'hold on' to their emotions in situations where it is not appropriate to express them. A poorly differentiated person, by comparison, may either be easily overtaken by emotional reactivity, or may shut down their emotions completely.

One of the unstated goals of psychotherapy is to nurture and improve the differentiation level of the client. This happens in the course of their resolving inner conflicts through the difficult and confronting work involved in the therapeutic process. Psychotherapy offers a very valid approach for a person interested in growing up and becoming a mature, well-defined, loving and responsive individual, and is courageous work.

While differentiation happens within the personality, it is intricately involved in our spiritual growth. 'Dying alive' improves our level of differentiation. The person who combines meditation with their own psychological work can make enhanced progress. It is unfortunate that these traditions have become separate and in some approaches quite alienated from each other, because both work towards the same ideal — a whole, content and empowered being. Any deliberate attempt to split human spiritual and psychological function seems problematic, indeed ill-conceived.

When we meditate and become soul-conscious, we move right out of the consciousness of the personality and gain a very different perspective of ourselves. It is rather like being on one side of a wall or the other, you cannot be on both sides at once. When we are soul-conscious, we are able to see ego-driven behaviour in the self, objectively. Being soul-conscious means it is impossible to experience emotions or any negativity at all, this is because we are experiencing our natural, essential states of being, such as peace, serenity or bliss. Likewise, when we are in the grip of ego-consciousness and emotional reactions, it is impossible to be soul-conscious and experience the peace and calm that is our natural state of being. We are born soul-conscious but reared and conditioned ego-conscious, a reality that causes a catastrophic split in consciousness in every one of us.

The process of changing consciousness in a complete, stable and permanent way involves 'dying alive'. Exchanging the consciousness of the ego for the higher consciousness of the soul is considered to be the most difficult thing for a human being to achieve, because it means completely letting go of the false self. The moment the soul says, 'I don't need you', the personality says, 'You'll die without me!' When the soul sees and experiences the destructiveness of a particular part of the personality, it can dissolve it immediately. This is the moment of 'dying alive'. In extreme cases the death itself can involve a catharsis emotionally and physically, such as deep, gut-wrenching sobs or an explosion into laughter or some other form of emotional release. On the other hand, it may be a very subtle melting experience into fluidity and softness. There are many parts to the human personality, and 'dying alive' ultimately involves the death of every part of us that is false. Meditation facilitates ego death with much greater ease than we might imagine.

After a few lessons in meditation, a prison inmate attending one of my groups announced that he was feeling very inspired by his morning and evening meditation sessions in his cell. I had just explained about the natural laws and how it is within our power to change our own innate tendencies and our fate, a subject which clearly fascinated him.

'I am going to change!' he announced to the group in an inspired

and very decisive manner. 'I am never going to come back to this place.'

When I arrived the following week he greeted me warmly, 'How's your karma, Jude?' he enquired. When I asked about his karma he was delighted.

'Improving,' he replied, 'I'm watching what I say and do. Remember I told you about the screw who gives me such a hard time? I'm really watching my reactions and I haven't retaliated once this week! The old impulses are still strong, but I'm meditating morning, afternoon and evening and it must be helping, because I'm not acting on those impulses, although I'm really aware of them.'

'That's wonderful!' I responded, genuinely delighted with the effort he was making. Each week he would greet me in the same way, 'How's your karma, Jude?' and we would go through our little welcome ritual, during which he would tell me how he had stopped reacting in certain tempting situations, or had managed to control the impulse to act in old, destructive ways.

Several weeks later I arrived for the group, but he did not rush to greet me in the usual way, instead he remained very quietly on the periphery. His head was hanging low and he would not look at me. I was curious. 'How's your karma?' I said after a while. He looked at me in silence, then spoke. 'Terrible,' he replied. I waited silently for an explanation. 'I might as well tell you,' he announced to the group. 'One of my duties here is to serve meals. I was serving dinner just before I came over here and a new inmate, I don't even know his name, asked me for more. "I'll pull your f...ing eyes out you greedy f...ing bastard!" I said. You should have seen the look on his face! He was in shock! Anyway, he took his plate and moved away very quickly.' The group was so silent you could hear a pin drop. 'I feel really bad about what I said to him. As soon as the group's over I think I'll try to find him and apologise.'

The following week he was back in his usual form. I asked whether he had followed up with the new inmate last week. 'Straight away,' he said, 'I found him after the group finished. I apologised, I told

him how sorry I was for what I'd said and you know what? This
really amazed me! He looked even more shocked when I apologised!
Then tears came into his eyes and he said, "Thank you, thank you for
finding me and saying that! It means a lot to me!" So I said, "You
mean there's no hard feelings?" "No," he answered, "no hard
feelings, thank you so much." I couldn't believe it! After apologising
I felt so much better!'

'Would you say this is new behaviour?' I asked. He smiled, 'Yes it
is, very new for me. But I feel so good about it! I really do know I can
change.'

Being vulnerable, feeling and human is not part of prison culture. Yet this inmate's conscience, once it began working, restored his integrity and spiritual function. His old defensive behaviour was no longer acceptable to him once he began meditating regularly and connecting with his conscience. Moreover, he was willing to 'die alive' in front of the group, which took a lot of courage. This is the power of awareness.

Once the soul realises the importance of letting go of the false ego, life situations and the people around us seem to conspire to reveal the parts of us that are phoney and incomplete, but they also reveal our progress. When the third eye opens, mirrors are everywhere. Spiritual change tends to speed up karmic settlement. Accounts will come thick and fast, affecting the body, mind, finances and relationships. Actually, people can wonder what has 'gone wrong' amid the seeming flurry of karmic activity that often gets triggered as the result of a spiritual awakening.

'Dying alive' is not something that happens once or twice, it is an ongoing part of spiritual growth. Accessing the compassion and clarity that come with soul-consciousness enables us to be clear yet gentle with ourselves. Attempts to dismantle the personality quickly are not recommended, nor is the violation of the self by unceremoniously digging for defects of character. Flawed and incomplete areas of the self will come to light naturally, often precipitated by external situations.

The soul pushes us into our inner work when we develop the inner resources to handle it, and have appropriate external support. Spiritually, we are deeply driven towards actualisation and fulfilment of our spiritual potential. This is the natural, healing movement of the soul, as it constantly encourages us to release and heal. Karma attracts the ideal situations and people for exposing the games and hidden aspects of our personality. As soon as the soul is witness, realisation hits like a thunderbolt, and that aspect of personality, now fully in awareness, can be finished. 'Dying alive' may involve feeling humiliated at times, but it gives way to birth and the joyous delivery of a new wholeness, which in itself can release a flow of ecstasy. This experience can also be earth shattering, but mostly it is quite subtle.

When someone begins meditating daily, their face changes within a few weeks. The eyes change too as the spirit is rekindled, sparkling with inner light. It does not take long for the effects of soul-consciousness to reveal a lightness and softening in the face and personality.

There are occasions when 'dying alive' is not a choice. While these occasions tend to be rare, they bear mentioning because they can be radical turning points. A time may come when the law of karma steps in to create a huge opportunity for growth, but it is disguised as loss. Rock-like armouring in the ego sometimes needs a heavy explosive to break it down, so a life situation will be perfectly manoeuvred to bring this about. This may occur through work, finances, family, personal life or friendships, but the scenario will be orchestrated to do the job very effectively. Furthermore, you will not be able to stop it happening or run away. When such a situation arises all you can do is surrender to it. Of course, internally you can always run away, but this has catastrophic repercussions in the long run. Such situations are a gift. From a soul-conscious perspective the drama that is your life is offering you the means to a massive breakthrough. The 'death' may be horribly painful, but for the soul who is willing to 'die alive', the rewards are great.

Like most things we do and become adept at doing, 'dying alive' and letting go become much easier with practice.

chapter ten

FACING *the*
SPIRITUAL VOID

Addictions and compulsions are one of the personality's ways of defending against feeling the emptiness of a spiritual void. So many of our defensive behaviours and emotional reactions do exactly the same thing. In the short term this may serve a purpose, but in the long term our defences take us very far away from ourselves. Exposing the void underneath our addictions and defences makes us feel extraordinarily vulnerable, with nowhere to hide. These voids may be the result of experiences in infancy and childhood, or later in life. Let us look at how they are formed.

One day, while swimming at the beach, I observed a small baby girl being placed on the sand near the water's edge by her mother, next to her brother who looked about two and a half years old. The older child was playing with his bucket and spade in an oddly concentrated fashion. He seemed as if in a trance, oblivious to everything around him. The mother put a bucket and spade in front of the baby and walked away, perhaps four or five metres from where the children sat. The baby stared after her mother showing no interest at all in the bucket, her sibling, the sand or the water. Calling out in baby babble, it was obvious that she just wanted her mother. Hearing her, her mother reacted by moving several paces further away and looking defiantly out to sea. Again, the baby called her mother, only to be consciously ignored. Eventually, the baby began to crawl towards her mother. Without looking, the woman seemed to sense this and moved further along the beach. As the baby girl reached closer, her mother moved away again, whereupon the baby stopped and just stared, in distress. The little one again made baby calls to get her mother's attention, and when this failed she continued crawling towards her mother again, this time reaching her feet. The woman picked the child up, took her briskly back to her brother and put her down on the sand, dumping the bucket and spade into her lap impatiently. The little boy seemed oblivious to his mother and baby sister through all of this. He was still playing with his bucket and spade, except I now detected he was playing intently, as opposed to happily, and appeared to have switched off and gone into his own safe little world somewhere.

The mother stalked even further down the beach this time, as the baby went through a similar ritual of staring after the woman and calling out. Finally, the baby crawled over to her mother's feet again, only to be ignored, and began to cry in deep, heart-broken sobs. The woman stared out to sea, unmoved and disinterested. By this time I was feeling quite devastated and decided I could bear no more. As I was deciding whether to leave, a man came running down the sand and picked the baby up. He appeared very distressed by the scene, and attempted to comfort the baby, who was by this time sobbing inconsolably for her mother. I left, noting the look of disbelief on the man's face as he stared at the woman (presumably his wife) dumbly, an unspoken question in his expression.

Babies, toddlers and young children are still soul-conscious. The purity, innocence, simplicity and joy of the soul shines brightly in the spiritual personality of an infant or child. There is no fear, anxiety or apprehension in the soul, until that is, these things are learned. Unfortunately, once rejection or abandonment enter a child's world, something very precious in the child is destroyed. When children experience hurt, especially by the principal carer, the loss of trust is devastating. Spiritually, these little beings begin to suffer at their core. Cut off from their essential, loving nature, the young child no longer experiences their inherent sense of trust, love and worth. She is initiated to the painful ego-conscious lesson, that 'love comes from outside' and furthermore, 'if it does not come from outside this means I am not loveable or deserving.' The inherent message is spiritually crippling.

Once the child is cut off from her own natural, inner state of spiritual love, a void or pocket of emptiness forms within the layer of personality that is created to cover the vulnerable wound. The void represents the loss of contact with their own essential love, and sooner or later she will feel driven to fill this void. Fear forms like a scab, protecting the wound from exposure. Since love is a basic need, as this child grows she will either learn to seek love, approval and praise from the outside, or utterly shun it. Making sure the void of love does not get exposed becomes little short of an art form, as defence mechanisms develop unconsciously around the voided area to ensure protection. She will probably learn to tie herself in knots to get the love and approval she longs for, from an outside source, because the void never feels full for long. Keeping a steady supply of love and approval on tap will be a major occupation. Alternatively she may try and stay safe, avoiding love and intimacy at all costs. If she is abandoned in love or rejected, which is likely to become a pattern for her, the original pain will be triggered and the spiritual void laid wide open.

When our emptiness is unmasked we can either find another person or thing to fill the void as soon as possible, or we can choose to feel the emptiness. The former will feel preferable, as the latter bring us into the pain we have been staving off. When we allow ourselves to feel the pain and grieve, however, we take a vital step towards healing and becoming free of the cycle of abandonment. Through meditation, an aware soul can move right into the void, discovering that there is really nothing to be afraid of. As spiritual light flows filling the void, it simply disappears. Dying alive means going through the fear and into the void, to re-emerge with complete freedom. After death comes birth, and a flood of released energy and healing.

Wherever there is a spiritual void there is an ego defence. Most of us have many such voids, and layers of defence covering them. We develop an automatic and unconscious ability to avert an encounter with our voids. For example, to deflect threatened exposure of the void, we will probably find an attachment to someone or something. Attachment breeds neediness, posses-siveness, anxiety, desire, anger, jealousy, obsession and fear, and usually a need to control. Only with awareness can we recognise the symptoms and make a decision not to act on the need, not to reach out for a 'filler' or a 'feel good'. Simply resisting such an urge exposes the void. Entering the void in a meditative state is the most powerful avenue of healing. In soul-consciousness the journey is not frightening, it is enlightening. Each void has its own story or memory of loss and by facing the void we bring it into awareness, where we can let go of it.

The loss or death of a loved one can have the effect of exposing many of our voids, suddenly and all at once. The pain can be intolerable — it can feel as though your heart or some other part of your body has been ripped out, and all that is left is a big emptiness. Our old ego identity and self-worth can vanish, leaving us at an emotional age somewhere between two and fifteen years.

The aftermath of a bereavement or loss can be reminiscent of being a toddler learning to walk again, as through deep grief we relive our developmental stages again. For example, if one's partner has died, we may have to learn to shop, cook, eat, survive, pay bills, buy or sell property, get a job and do things all on our own — all over again. Even though being thrown into the void is painful, the best thing we can do is embrace it fully and allow our tears and grief to support our healing, as they inevitably will. A deep and personal loss provides an opportunity to grow, to experience the voids we have unconsciously been filling with another person or situation, and to find our true value within the loss. The fear that ordinarily stops us encountering our voids is less of an issue when we lose a loved one because the impact of the loss thrusts us through it anyway. Being able to recognise the void as a place where we may heal and awaken spiritually enables us to embrace this very important work. To undergo such an experience means to emerge from it a deeper, more authentic, aware, and expanded being who is able to reach out to others with compassion and empathy.

Many people who experience a significant and personal loss in their lives may find themselves instinctively searching for spiritual comfort, and a spiritual understanding of their loss. Questions about the meaning of existence and God can arise, opening up new frontiers of spiritual enquiry. Turning to a Higher Source at such times, in a heartfelt personal sense, and inviting this Being into the deep, hollow spaces inside, takes the healing of grief to a new level. Here is the only source of true fullness. Making meaning of our losses and life experiences is a significant part of the spiritual journey.

The period that follows letting go is said to be a time of sanctity and grace. Freedom and release flow, bringing a feeling of aliveness and wholeness. 'Dying alive' means that with every void we embrace, it is much easier to be soul-conscious. As our falseness dissolves, our true spiritual nature reveals itself. The more willing we are to 'die', the more alive, real and free we become.

chapter eleven

POWER *and*

TRANSFORMATION

As the soul moves through its journey of transformation, an exchange occurs. Whenever a part of the ego is successfully relinquished, a spiritual quality or ability that was hidden automatically takes its place.

When the subject of letting go of our ego defences arises, people have often expressed their concern to me that leaving the soul undefended and vulnerable to attack is not an attractive option. Naturally enough, put this way, it is not, but dropping ego defences is only part of the picture. Once we begin meditating, our consciousness undergoes a subtle and gradual change over time, as we shift from ego-consciousness to soul-consciousness. As this shift occurs our ego defences are naturally dissolved, but they are replaced by something that enables us to participate in life much more effectively. They are replaced by our original spiritual qualities and powers, and as with anything new, we have to become aware of them and learn how to use them. Using the spiritual powers instead of ego defences can be a source of real inspiration to the self and others, and they may come into our awareness in the strangest of ways.

One evening, soon after launching an ongoing weekly program for people in recovery from addictions, I was feeling unsure of myself and quietly hoping that no one would turn up for the session. As fate would have it an unusually large number of people turned up. On this particular night I became aware that quite a few people in the room were 'on the nod', meaning they had used either methadone or heroin before coming and were quite drugged. When we paused for meditation, several of them stretched right out on the floor and nodded off completely. The room was a generous size without losing intimacy, and it was packed with people. I sat at the front leading meditation, my thoughts anything but meditative. All I could focus on was the unmistakable pall of stale cigarette smoke clinging to people's clothes, grubby feet, and sleeping bodies. 'Why am I doing this?' I asked myself, 'I must be mad!' Then something happened. My stage of yoga became extraordinarily intense as I felt a powerful presence enter my body. Then I experienced a sensation as though my heart were opening, pouring out love like a great river. Two great arms seemed to reach out from my heart stretching right around the room, embracing every single person in the room. It felt as though these subtle arms were lifting everyone into my heart and loving them unconditionally with a deeply intense, powerful, unlimited love. My heart seemed to be holding and uplifting the entire room and everyone in it. I had never felt such utterly sweet, gentle, pure love. The meditation seemed timeless as I received my lesson without words: when love and the Power to Tolerate is lacking, the ego judges and criticises. I had a lot to learn about spiritual love and my lessons were only just beginning. How can we truly love another — let alone ourselves   if we cannot tolerate their flaws? My new teachers, it seemed, had arrived, and as I entered one of the most meaningful and pivotal chapters in my life, the love that I was now experiencing left me in no doubt that I was precisely where I was meant to be.

Without spiritual love, I do not believe the soul has the wherewithal to bring about deep and lasting change. Love is power and it makes anything possible. Laying my ego defences to rest is an act of love and surrender, but in their place I must learn to use my spiritual powers as a healthy means of coping with life situations and in all my interactions with others.

In the transformational journey, eight principal expressions of spiritual power replace the ego defences and they are meant to be used, for they protect the soul from the games of the personality (my own and other people's) and are a source of great empowerment. The combination of spiritual knowledge and yoga develops the ability to concentrate the intellect. From this intense concentration, a powerful discrimination arises and the various powers spring from this. The primary powers are: to Discern, to Decide, to Tolerate, to Withdraw, to Accommodate, to Pack Up, to Face, to Co-operate.

To begin with, the *Power to Discern* endows intuitive knowledge of what is truth, what is right, what is aligned with spiritual purpose and what is otherwise, so that a question cannot even arise in my mind. With this power, confusion, illusion or delusion — all defences employed by the personality — are unable to mask the truth. This ability to discern then facilitates the *Power to Decide*. Decisions can have wide and far-reaching implications, so the Power to Decide is grounded in a spiritual perception of people, circumstances and what is required, coupled with a clear vision of the karmic consequences of decisions that are made.

Spiritual growth tends to happen when we are pushed into areas in which we either feel unsure of ourselves or feel downright uncomfortable, so the *Power to Tolerate* is essential. For example, it is important to be able to self-validate and tolerate criticism and adverse opinion rather than clinging to a need for approval from others, in order to maintain healthy boundaries. People-pleasing and needing to be liked are ego defences, and if I transfer this behaviour to the spiritual path, the Power to Tolerate will not develop. When I am bathing in the warm glow of others' praise and regard, I need to be equally detached from this, too. The very same qualities some people respect and like about me, others may reject. Other people's opinion of me, whether positive or negative, should not influence me.

On the other hand, being sensitive and always needing to

have things 'just right' or the way I want, reveals a lack of tolerance. It also means spending much of my existence either unhappy or keeping others at a distance. The *Power to Tolerate* is pivotal to being discerning and truthful about what motivates my every action. It is the essence of being real but as long as I am influenced by what others think of me, even very subtly, it will not inform my actions. Once I do begin to grow spiritually I will need to tolerate the difference that begins to emerge between me and other people in my life. To tolerate does not mean to 'put up with', but 'to suffer no ill effects from' — like tolerating penicillin.

The *Power to Withdraw* is very much to do with respecting my own limits or boundaries, in maintaining a strong self-focus. As far as the personality is concerned, tempting situations abound in life. The ability to withdraw means to refrain from 'fixing' others, giving advice, or otherwise involving myself in situations that are non-productive, or in which I have no business to be involved — even if invited. This power enables me to enjoy healthy relationships and involvements that result from clear, respectful boundaries.

The *Power to Accommodate* nourishes acceptance of what is. Changing circumstances and inner transition can be very challenging. The personality naturally resists and defends against transition, change, or anything that challenges the ego; whereas the soul flows with the prevailing conditions, accommodating whatever circumstances occur, adjusting immediately. There is a saying that when things go wrong or do not happen as planned, 'children blame, whereas an adult will say, "What must I do to make the best of this situation?"' The Power to Accommodate allows me to enjoy difference and remain easy going when the unexpected occurs, as I develop the ability to adjust and act appropriately, rather than resist change.

The *Power to Pack Up* enables me to finish a train of thought in an instant. Whether it be personal concerns, worrying situations, or just intrusive thoughts, the Power to Pack Up finishes mental business that is non-productive. Worrying never solves anything, nor does it promote positive feelings. Waste thoughts drain energy from the soul. With this power, I can stop my thoughts in a second and regain a state of inner equilibrium and peace.

The *Power to Face* speaks of my ability to embrace truth and fear and to relinquish control. Supreme acts of surrender carry rich rewards, the main one being freedom. The personality seeks to defend itself through denial, avoidance, excuses, manipulation and games, but with the Power to Face when untoward events happen I face them squarely and deal with them. Holding on when it is time to let go, or letting go when I need to hold on, is ego force. Using the Power to Face means 'surrender to reality and fly'.

The *Power to Co-operate* involves having the resources to transcend individualism and participate in a task that is for the greater good. Service often involves the Power to Co-operate, when many people are needed to bring a project to fruition. No matter how talented or skilled the individuals in the group, they will not get the job done if they are unable to transcend their egos and work in harmony. The ego may feel a need to criticise or may want things done a certain way, but this creates disruption. Whatever the task, there is the understanding that being able to harmonise with others, focus on and learn from the process is what is important, for the outcome is always in the hands of God.

While there are many more powers that accompany spiritual growth, these eight principal powers provide a focus. They also work together. Discrimination is always required to know which power is appropriate. It is useless to employ the Power to Withdraw when the Power to Face is required to deal with a life situation. Using the Powers instead of ego defences is a different way of being in the world. The mind of a yogi soul becomes very powerful through the discipline that arises from meditation, and from transcending the ego defences.

Transformation of the personality and ego defences is not as great a hardship as the ego-personality would have us believe. Once we begin to accumulate spiritual power and develop our natural awareness through meditation, we will begin to deal with our defences, addictions and unresolved emotional baggage as a matter of course. In fact, much of the time it is barely detectable. With a regular, ongoing practice of meditation, we notice the gentle dissolution of negative traits and a reshaping of the original beauty of the soul. As a sculptor works with a block of marble, removing its flaws and revealing the unique markings and natural beauty of the stone, so the Supreme Soul works, very lovingly, with us.

chapter twelve

YESTERDAY, TODAY
and TOMORROW

The soul's field of karma is the Earth, where we enter the world of matter, relationships and entropy. It is here that we enter the physical dimension and the construct of time, within which we can evaluate and measure our lives. As the soul takes rebirth over a span of time, the fullness and power of our lifeforce or energy, the hallmark of a radiant and divine being, imperceptibly dwindles. At a certain point the spiritual personality fades and the ego-personality begins to replace it. The memory of the soul's original beauty and divinity also fades, as the ego-personality takes over more and more, birth after birth. Understanding the soul's journey through a span of time is the key that unlocks the mystical and mysterious story of the human spirit. Energy moves from a usable to an unusable state, and the soul is energy, as is the earth, rocks, trees, plants, ocean, rain and light. Everything is living energy.

My first encounter with the theory of cyclic time proved extremely vexatious. Although I did not realise it immediately, my world view had been shattered. The idea of an exactly repeating cycle was something I preferred not to think about, yet I would think about it frequently and lament to my closest friends, 'I can't believe I have to go through (such and such) again!' Soon they too, were lamenting certain aspects of their own lives and saying similar things to me! Eventually I put it all aside, deciding to focus on the aspects of spiritual knowledge that really worked well for me. After a while it ceased to be an issue.

From antiquity, the world view had been that the passing of time represented regress. The Roman theologians embraced a linear theory of time moving progressively towards decay, whereas the Greek philosophers and other ancient traditions understood time to proceed in a cyclic fashion, moving regressively from an apex or Golden Age, which came to a metaphoric end when Pandora lifted the lid on the box containing the evils of life. After the Golden Age came the Silver, Copper and Heroic ages, that finally plunge into a state of total decadence, the Iron Age. This cycle took some thousands of years to complete, ending in chaos. As energy reaches it's lowest point the deity souls return, restoring divine order and perfection on Earth.

Similarly, the Hindus embrace a cycle of four ages: Gold, Silver, Copper and Iron. At the apex of their cycle is a Golden age, a time of earthly perfection which degrades as time moves through the Silver, Copper and Iron ages, descending into chaos and destruction at the close of the Iron Age. As with the ancient Greeks, the Hindu culture has a colourful and entertaining array of stories about, and religious practices based on, their deities. Within these stories are powerfully symbolic themes of the struggle between darkness and light, flesh and spirit, essence and ego, truth and falsehood, good and evil, devil and deity.

The various ages of the cycle combine to present a picture which is balanced between the light of the Golden Age, and the darkness of the Iron Age. Between the Iron and Golden ages is a very brief transitional period called the Diamond or Confluence Age, so named since it marks the transition between one cycle and another. The Diamond Age is significant as a time when all information becomes available, when all that is false is exposed and truth can no longer be hidden. We are currently living in the Diamond Age.

Having been raised with the theory of linear time, I realised how I had taken this world view for granted, until it was challenged. Reviewing world history, it is evident how powerful a particular world view can be, especially when that view is assumed, generationally and by all society, to be the truth. One of the most obvious examples of this comes from the mediaeval Christians who believed that the Sun revolved around the Earth. When Galileo publicly stated what he, Copernicus and others had worked out, that the Earth revolved around the Sun, the Roman Church threatened to behead him unless he recanted. Even though he recanted, he was branded a heretic and kept under house arrest until he died. His crime? He challenged the world view of the presiding power!

Throughout history, world views have changed in response to new knowledge. The mechanistic philosophy has been preoccupied with controlling nature, since, like God, nature possesses a will of its own. God was not so easy to control and was therefore marginalised. In the late eighteenth and early nineteenth centuries, as the Industrial Revolution swept through Europe, new scientific and technological inventions radically transformed the way the workforce, society and the family functioned. For example, the work of Francis Bacon, René Descartes and Isaac Newton helped create a new vision of the world between 1620, when Bacon's work *Novum Organum* was published, and the 1850s. These men captivated Europe, convincing society that their ideas, as a new organising principle for the world, were the way of the future. Thus, the mechanistic world view was born. But perhaps the greatest challenge for this new world order was human beings, who, because of their emotions, simply could not be trusted to behave in a controlled and predictable way — unlike machines.

Around 1750 the radical notion of 'progress' in world history took birth. Our current world is a product of that thinking. This new world view presented time as linear, but moving towards perfection rather than decay. With all the new inventions, labour-saving devices, technological and scientific advances that are a product of the machine age, certainly there has been progress at one level. We have clever machines, that, at the press of a button entertain us, raise us to the top of a building, cook our food or wash our clothes. However, the question must be asked: is the human race progressing or is science and technology providing a veneer of 'progress'?

Where have the mechanistic ideals of controlling nature got us? Our natural environment is irrevocably damaged and nature is screaming. The world view we were raised on has betrayed us, yet who clings to it? Economists, corporations, politicians, governments, manufacturers, industrialists, scientists and world leaders. Sadly, this duality underpins the established structures of our civilisation.

A new way of understanding the current effects of industrial-isation came about in 1868 when the seeds of another 'new' world view were sown. Entropy was defined and named by the German physicist, Rudolf Clausius. After much debate, the entropy law has taken a highly regarded position in modern science. The Law of Entropy is the second law of thermody-namics which states that all energy moves from order into chaos, or from a usable form into an unusable form. Jeremy Rifkin's exploration of the entropy law, in his book *Entropy*,[16] examines the idea that this law overturns the mechanistic theory that time moves increasingly towards perfection, and supports the Greek and Hindu cycles of time. In our current high-entropy culture, Rifkin states, massive energy consumption is the cost of our materialist, indulgent, consumerist society. If many scientists and progressive thinkers are correct in believing there is a fixed amount of energy in the universe and that we are currently approaching an important time when the entropic effect will reach completion, then this also means we are running out of time. Time, energy and entropy it appears, are inextricably linked.

The Greeks and Hindus have remembered their deities as a master race, possessing qualities and powers that have been long lost in our civilisation. If such beings never existed could they have been remembered and worshipped with such fervour and endurance until today, thousands of years after their Golden Age reign? Ruins of the Harappan civilisation, thought to date back 4000 years and discovered in the Indus Valley in what is now Pakistan, reveal a level of sophistication in their bathrooms and plumbing that aligns them with modern trends in cleanliness and hygiene. Like the Harappan civilisation, other civilisations of antiquity such as the ancient Egyptians, Greeks and Romans had a much lower rate of entropy than we do.

The *Mahabharata*, written two and a half thousand years ago, depicts a great war between two families of cousins who are fighting over their kingdom, a war in which both sides describe possessing a weapon of mass destruction that they ultimately resort to using. 'The secret of this weapon has never been revealed. It could pierce the heart of the world, it could even kill the gods.' Even though written two and a half thousand years ago, the description of: 'a white heat ... men, animals, the Earth itself — all are shrivelling to ashes', is recognisably that of a nuclear explosion. The *Mahabharata* and *Bhagavad Gita*, both foremost Hindu scriptures, are considered by many a scholar to be a symbolic treatise on our own civilisation in the twenty-first century.

The ancient palaces of India were not constructed with air conditioning or technologically advanced features. In place of these are architectural and design features that have been so well thought out that they utilise natural aspect and light, breezes, scented flora and natural running water, to provide low-tech cooling and heating as well as creating a beautiful energy and atmosphere. Their use of building and furnishing materials, and environmental position, ensure beautiful and comfortable living. Summer palaces and winter palaces have been designed for the seasons and for maximum comfort. The ancients of India lived in a way that created a very slow rate of entropy, and as with the other ancient civilisations, their appreciation of beauty, art and the use of non-energy consuming, non-polluting natural resources in their designs, buildings and city planning, put them way ahead of modern civilisation.

Ideas that informed the Industrial Revolution and which govern our world today, such as 'time is linear, represents progress and moves increasingly towards perfection', are unsustainable. Our civilisation has barely reached the technological or scientific sophistication that has existed in the past. Our dollar-driven, high-entropy society is blinding itself to human values, while the wheel of time appears to be moving into its lowest point, into what is described in the last chapter of the *Mahabharata* as 'The Final Illusion'. Those who have not conquered themselves are depicted living indulgently in the delusion that they are in heaven, when they are actually in hell; whereas the heroes of the *Mahabharata* 'melt on the mountain' in a symbolic act of total surrender to God.

ॐ

The cyclic understanding of time and energy reveals an overall movement from a very low-entropy, spiritually advanced and elevated race of beings, to our current, energetically degraded world.

The regenerating and repeating cycles of the Greeks and Hindus fit comfortably with the fact that our seasons, the movement of the planets in the solar system, and even our body rhythms, occur in cycles. Linear time moving towards either decay or perfection does not acknowledge that which seems obvious: everything in nature is cyclical. It appears that a non-linear thinking mind created us, nature and our physical world. Could it be that as the soul moves from order into chaos, spiritually, so the world of matter and nature follow? Hesiod, the Greek poet and historian, describes the Iron-Aged condition:

For now in these latter days is the Race of Iron. Never by day shall they rest from travail and sorrow, and never by night from the hand of the spoiler. The father shall not be of one mind with the children, nor the children with the father, nor the guest with the host that receives them, nor friends with friends ... Parents shall swiftly age and swiftly be dishonoured ... The righteous man or the good man or he that keeps his oath shall not find favour, but they shall honour rather the doer of wrong and the proud man insolent. Right shall rest in might of hand and truth shall be no more.[17]

and the Golden-Aged condition:

In the beginning, a golden race of mortal men was made by the immortal dwellers on Olympus ... They lived like Gods with hearts free from care, without part or lot in labour or sorrow.
Pitiful old age did not await them, but ever the same in strength of hand and foot, they took their pleasure in feasting apart from all evils.
When they died it was as though they were overcome by sleep. All good things were theirs and the grain harvest was yielded by bountiful earth of her own accord — abundantly, ungrudgingly — while they in peace and goodwill lived upon their lands with good things in abundance.[18]

The spiritual indications are that the human soul is being readied for a great and imminent change. As energy speeds up, entropy speeds up. This feels as if time, which is really just a mental construct, is moving more and more rapidly, as we hurtle towards this change. Today, the word 'transformation' has come into common usage. Is it the case that people have always talked of spiritual transformation the way they do now? The time has come to embrace new thinking for the future. As challenging as bringing about a new world order may seem, it will happen anyway. It is unstoppable, and will not be brought about by international power brokers or leaders of the current world order. The new world order requires a new state of being and the ability to be very subtle. Rigidly clinging to the old secure, measurable mechanistic world of Newton will not prevent change occurring, it will just mean being left behind.

The soul which has been part of a Garden of Eden, a Golden Age or a Heaven on Earth has been in a state of exalted fullness and spiritual endowment, a state of such perfection that it is unknown in our current civilisation — in our Iron Age. Nature then, has also been through a time of perfection, fullness and immaculate beauty. Many may denounce such notions as fantasy, but the fact is, if the soul is empty now, it must have been full at one time. The soul cannot lose what it has never had. The Greeks based their drama on stories of their gods. Mount Olympus figures prominently, symbolising the 'highest place' from which the gods came. It is evident from Greek and Hindu drama, philosophy and history, that both cultures remembered a race of superior beings and a time preceding theirs, when the world order was one of perfection. Plato and Aristotle were so mindful of the process of increasing decay over time, they placed a high premium on maintaining minimal change in order to preserve as much stability in society and in the culture, as possible. It seems from Hesiod's account that the souls of the Golden Age experienced a beautiful, flowing interaction of essential qualities, and communication at an exalted level of consciousness and heart and soul evolution. They do not age, become tired or infirm and they do not know suffering or death because they live in peace, in accord with nature and the divine order.

What a contrast a world where heart and divinity are sovereign, compared to the left brain, 'mind over matter', cognitive, materialistic, mechanistically driven world of today.

The Golden and Silver ages are remembered (there is no documented history) as a time of unity, oneness and harmony on Earth. When the soul is spiritually powerful, the shift to external wielding of force is unknown. As an old French proverb says, 'happy people do not make history.' As we approach the final days of the Iron Age, the time of greatest spiritual disempowerment, demonstrations of power are linked with the ego, not the soul. Spiritual wholeness and an elevated culture are distinguished by equality and inclusion. Polarisation, male superiority, minority groups and power differentials — the great afflictions of the late twentieth and early twenty-first centuries — are a symptom of a civilisation that has lost its way.

The final days of the Iron Age are dwindling and a shifting consciousness heralds inevitable change. The new world order is being established, and when the degraded energy of this world connects with the high vibration of the new, a spontaneous and instant reversal of energy will occur, bringing about the rebirth of matter.

It is time to turn quietly inward, away from the noise and distraction of the cognitive mind and the world drama. It is time to be slow and present, to return to the solitude and serenity of spirit, where the self and God may be linked in a deep and pure love. It is time to return to the dimension of silence, to our true consciousness, and remember who we are, a peaceful and eternal being of light.

As the sun sets on the 'progress' of the machine age: global warming, environmental devastation, greenhouse emissions, poisoned waterways and natural calamities, the final moments of the Iron Age will end. Through the cool mists of a new, peaceful sunrise, the Golden Age will be unveiled and a new age resonant with perfection and splendour will dawn.

part two

COMMUNION

chapter thirteen

CONTEMPLATION

Finding a spiritual path that feels right can be a wonderful beginning, as a new and exciting way of being opens up to us. Embracing our path for the long haul, however, means making great adjustments, as all the various aspects of our lives must gradually be brought into alignment with our changing consciousness and spiritual way of being. What is set in motion by simply contemplating the self can result in a completely transformed human being and a transformed life. The power of transformation is such that we cannot continue to live an ordinary life in an ordinary way. When we change the world changes, and when enough of us change, the world too, will undergo great and positive change, as nature and our natural environment change — reflecting this change in human consciousness.

Our early steps along this path begin with contemplation of 'I' the soul, then, as many who have taken up the spiritual path experience, we must begin to find our way in society as an aware, awakened, soul-conscious and contemplative being. This is to 'be in the world, not of it', doing much the same things but in a higher consciousness. The contemplative soul brings their peaceful state into the physical world. Awareness focused within is self-contemplation. Contemplation is the movement into soul-consciousness which prepares the soul for yoga, or union. This movement involves one significant challenge, the undisciplined mind is driven to contrive waste thoughts to sabotage a connection with self. Rather than struggling to control intrusive thoughts, it is easier to focus on a deeper place where the heart speaks its own language of feelings. Without feelings, the attempt at yoga or union is cognitive, rather than an experience of connection. A relationship without love and spiritual attraction will break easily. Yoga is like this. When the heart engages, the soul shifts into a flow of super-sensuous connection.

A contemplative being searches for answers within rather than without. Yoga reconnects us with our ability to tap into our true spiritual resources through which we experience truth and enlightened understanding. We can begin by learning to alter our consciousness through meditation. Raja Yoga meditation is best learnt from a teacher rather than from a book, as it is experiential. The effects are quite subtle to begin with, but as the soul stirs into wakefulness, each day something new unfolds within. It is like watching a baby discover new things with each day that passes. The best times to meditate are first thing in the morning and last thing at night. Religious and spiritual traditions through the ages have recognised the hours between two and five am as the best time to pray or meditate. Known as the 'hour of nectar' this time is especially good because the vibrations are at their least degraded. Making meditation your first experience of the day is what is important, whatever time of day this may be.

An open mind is essential. Spiritual knowledge can challenge the ego-personality and may take some time to digest, while altering consciousness is such a subtle experience that early attempts may leave you feeling that nothing much is happening. Trying to control the mind is not meditation, it is impossible. If you try to meditate with your 'head' or rational mind, it will feel laborious and will not work, but when you channel your energy away from the mind and into the heart then just allow yourself to feel, the door will open.

The mind–body connection comes into focus when we meditate, and the effect of the state of the body on the mind becomes highlighted. While it is not necessary to follow a particular diet in order to learn meditation, it is worth mentioning that the body must be free from mind and mood-altering substances and chemicals when meditating, as they block our ability to alter our consciousness in a natural way. Even having a lot of caffeine in your system over stimulates the central nervous system, which prevents concentration. While many people decide they want to become vegetarian and possibly change other aspects of their lifestyle once they have begun meditating, the decision is an entirely personal one. Many people experience a marked loss of interest in meat, alcohol, nicotine and other drugs when they meditate regularly. However, changes are internally generated and happen in a natural way, as a consequence of a change in consciousness. Being soul-conscious has a flow-on effect and, in time, the soul expresses clear distaste for habits and activities that are not in tune with its spiritual nature. Using force to bring about change does not work long-term, whereas real change springs from the heart and is spiritually generated. Discipline in the true sense is an action motivated by love, not by control or force.

There are some common myths about meditation. Some people claim they meditate while reading the morning paper or watching television. It must be said that shifting into a higher consciousness is quite distinct from reading or from watching television. Another myth is that meditation requires you to stop thinking and make the mind blank. Actually, no one can stop their mind from thinking, it is not possible. While you are awake, and for periods during sleep, the mind is actively working. Channelling energy away from the cognitive mind, in itself, makes us feel more peaceful. When we meditate regularly our energy slows, allowing us to be present in the moment, and there is a drastic reduction in waste thoughts. No matter how busy the mind is, with practice, we can make it slow and calm through the experience of self-contemplation. When the soul turns its awareness onto itself, there is an instant feeling of peace.

All living things have a life force of their own beyond their biological existence. Clearly, there is a divine order to nature and to all existence. Different species have separate and unique characteristics and behaviours, so that dandelion seeds scattered in the wind will produce dandelions that look and behave like dandelions. Tomato seeds will produce tomatoes that look and behave like tomatoes. Animals and insects have souls, even plants and rocks, as living things, have a type of soul. Mosquitoes always behave like mosquitoes and elephants always behave like elephants. Just as human souls always reincarnate as humans, a plant is always a plant and an insect always an insect. In keeping with this divine and natural order, the soul carries innate traits and nature related to its particular species. Thus a spiritual migration of soul from one kingdom to another would create a wilder and more chaotic scenario than anything science fiction or Woody Allen could ever dream up. The natural order has been created by a perfect being. This is something to meditate on.

Entropic forces appear to govern time, so that as entropy increases it becomes a principal distinction between past and future. The soul has an apparently discrete entropy which governs the soul's journey from a state of full empowerment to emptiness. When spiritual power is significantly discharged, it is time for the soul to realise itself once more and recharge. As the soul increasingly realises itself and recharges, the more its discrete entropy is reversed, returning the soul to the empowered or complete state once more. Imagine what might happen when a significant number of souls are very close to achieving this. What effect might they have on the world?

Anyone can meditate wherever, whenever and however they want to, in isolation or with others. There are no 'musts' or 'shoulds'. If a soul experiences a calling to the spiritual path, this means connecting with others who have chosen the same path and who provide a frame of reference, empathy and companionship. In this sense, community is simply a part of the journey. However, it is not necessary to be in a closed community, separate from society. Spirituality is something that is practised in everyday life and integrated in every part of our lives. It is not something that is done exclusively at certain times in certain places, with certain people. Spirituality is an integral aspect of human existence, and flows through our work, family life, and all of our connections, relationships and activities. Otherwise, a spiritual practice cannot be said to have integrity. Abandoning dependants and family responsibilities to sit on a mountain for the rest of our life is not what 'being spiritual' is about.

Spiritual growth blossoms when we face the tests and challenges in our everyday life, not when we avoid them. It is our consciousness that must change, not our environment or the people and situations around us. Connecting with others who share the journey also provides an opportunity for learning, for spiritual reflection and for communion. Spiritual growth is an aspect of human development that fosters the highest levels of self-support and self-responsibility, as well as the ability to be in true community with others. Meditation is a natural way to embrace and nurture our deeper spiritual instincts and connections with one another.

Time and space seem to alter with meditation. Perhaps 'just being' seems to slow down the moment, but when our energy slows down the mind can become still, and we exist fully in the moment, in our 'inner space', gaining a sense of separation from the physical world and its dramas. Contemplation nourishes the intellect, allowing us to immerse ourselves in the esoteric world of the spirit more deeply over time. However, spiritual gain does mean loss at other levels. Aspects of the self that are false are sacrificed in service of soul. Ego identity, which has defined us, our relationships and how we handle our existence over a long time, no longer offers a valid definition. Later we recognise these sacrifices as small matters. They are stories of the soul, and the soul has many stories, but self-mastery is the ultimate story and it is one of daring, courage, transformation and communion. It reveals the passage from darkness into enlightenment, of coming to know and value the self and life with the passion and wisdom that arise from knowing the dark and the light. Until we have fully experienced the darkness, we cannot fully understand the light. The light that shines in the eyes of a yogi brings light into the world. The contemplative being resides in the same body as it did before its transformation, works in the same job, interacts with the same people, but has shifted inwardly, living and being in a consciousness which is transforming. In this way, the journey of life changes.

chapter fourteen

VALUES

As the soul is drawn progressively along the spiritual path and into the aware state of being, our perception of everything undergoes subtle, continuous change. Following the spiritual path means adjustment is a constant in our lives. Our values begin to change within the first twelve months, and within the second year our values will usually have altered quite dramatically. The reason for this is that as our consciousness gently transforms from the ego-centred state to the soul-centred state, we are becoming a different person — an increasingly real person. The false values of the ego-personality fall away naturally and are replaced by the true values of the soul.

Valuing ourselves and one another as spiritual beings means spiritual values form the basis of our existence, no matter who or where we are. When we relate to others in the consciousness of ego rather than soul, our connections become degraded and phoney. The ideal of our modern mechanistic world is a 'value-free' society, and hand-in-hand with this ideal comes increasingly large correctional institutions, policing organisations, and levels of anti-social and pathological behaviour.

Some years after I started working for Corrective Services, a man in his late twenties joined a group I was facilitating. A few days after he arrived he introduced himself and made it clear that he had been in and out of correctional settings since his early teens. He added that almost three years had passed since his last release. He would not be in for long, he assured me, as his misdemeanour was from years ago and very minor. Tim (I will call him) expressed himself extremely well. He was bright, articulate, and wanted to be regarded as someone who had reformed himself.

'This place has really gone downhill since I was last here,' he volunteered. I asked him to explain. 'The values have disintegrated,' he said, 'it used to be that people in here had consideration for each other. When I went for a shower yesterday after I arrived, I could not get a towel. The system in here is that someone is rostered to look after towels and so on, and it used to be that when you first arrived you'd be issued with a towel and soap straightaway. Not now, not here! Little things like that are important in a place like this, but when I asked for a towel yesterday the person responsible didn't want to know. I've been here two days and I still don't have a towel! What has happened to this place? Just because this is gaol doesn't mean we can't treat each other like human beings!'

Tim went on, 'There used to be a better class of crim in this place — more consideration,' he added, 'thankfully, I'm only here for three weeks, and that's it, I won't be coming back. I've got a good job now and a girl I'm going to marry. I'm straight, I've got a life, and I don't need any more of this!'

Tim had brought the focus onto a loss of values in prison culture. I was well aware that during the years I had been connected with this world an observable deterioration had occurred, just as Tim noted. Prison may be one of the last places on earth, some might think, where values could be of importance, but while Tim was sharing his observations of prison culture with the group, another inmate, Nick, who had spent much of his adult life in gaol, also began to lament the loss of values in prison culture. 'It's not like it was in the 'eighties', *he concluded, 'there's a different type of crim in here now.'*

The groups were open to inmates who were serving the final three years of their sentence. Nick was due for release in twelve months and he stayed with the group for about nine months. Nick had a serious, long-term alcohol problem and was an engaging, sweet, ingenuous, rather child-like soul who would take umbrage if other group members suggested that only drug addicts supported their

*habit with crime. 'I've always supported my drinking with crime,'
he would chip in, with a rather quiet hint of pride, 'and I've never
used a drug in my life!' I suspected he had some alcohol-related
brain damage and suggested to him that his regular stints in gaol,
providing forced abstinence, were the best thing that could have
happened to him. He had been sober for the length of his sentence
(several years), but it was obvious that he would be straight back to
the bars when he was released from prison. He had more drinking to
do — he knew it and I knew it! I worked relentlessly on his denial,
regardless. With three months of his sentence remaining he left the
group, returning to say goodbye just before his release. He had
confided to me about his past criminal activities, so in parting, I
extracted a promise from him that he would not cross the Harbour
Bridge (to my side of it) to commit crime. Oddly enough, he took me
seriously and agreed.*

*About a year later I was in Sydney's eastern suburbs when someone
called to me in the street and came running after me. It was Nick.
He seemed pleased to see me. We chatted for a while and suddenly
he said, 'I've kept my promise to you, Jude, I haven't crossed the
Harbour Bridge to do any jobs.' I felt oddly touched. Then he offered
me a case of wine, pointing to a large station wagon loaded with
boxes of wine.*

*'I don't drink, Nick,' I answered cheerfully, 'or receive stolen
goods.' A quiet glimmer of a smile flashed in his eyes momentarily.
'It's a very good vintage, I'd like to give you a nice Christmas
present.'*

*'No thanks Nick,' I said firmly. The hint of a quiet inner smile
flashed through his expression again.*

*'Merry Christmas Jude, it's really good to see you. I'll see you again
some time.' With that, he jumped into his station wagon and disappeared.*

*One evening about eighteen months later Nick bounced into the
room for group with the other inmates, greeting me warmly. 'I've
been looking forward to coming back into your group,' he said, with*

quiet enthusiasm. He seemed very pleased to be back with us, although he announced proudly that he had stayed out of gaol for two and a half years. In or out of gaol, Nick seemed to be happy. He managed the prison culture extremely well (after spending so much time in it) and was genuinely liked by inmates and staff. After another two-and-a-half-year drinking spree I suspected he was a little more 'knocked-off' (brain-damaged) than before, although not as badly as I might have predicted.

Around the time of Nick's return a new inmate joined the group, a gentle person in his late forties, who I will call Harry. Harry was a 'new chum' and still suffering from the culture shock of coming into prison. I asked him to introduce himself and tell us why he had come to the group. He said he felt a certain stigma in coming to a drug and alcohol group because he did not have a problem with either, but one of the counsellors had encouraged him to come along. He explained that this was his first time in prison and that he should never have come to gaol — which triggered a ripple of laughter! Harry was a well educated white collar criminal who had succumbed to temptation handling very large sums of other people's money through the company he worked for. He covered his tracks carefully, but was ultimately framed by police, he claimed, on possession of drugs, a fact which utterly incensed Harry because he had never used or dealt drugs in his life. Harry had a good criminal lawyer working on his case and was certain he would be out of gaol, with charges dropped, in a couple of months.

In the meantime, the group proved an eye-opener for Harry, especially when he was introduced to the notion that he actually did have an addiction — to other people's money! One night Nick was sharing his drinking history, and when he finished Harry got up from his chair, walked over to him, and placed a fatherly hand on his shoulder.

'I'm really concerned about your drinking, Nick,' he said quietly, looking steadily into Nick's eyes. Nick seemed to be in shock. Some weeks later, Nick arrived early for group and told me that Harry

would often approach him in the yard and say, 'I'm very worried about your drinking, Nick.'

'No one has ever cared about my drinking,' Nick added, 'but Harry does.' Over the course of the following year both men continued in the group, developing an interaction that began having a curiously positive effect on Nick.

When Harry had been in gaol for almost a year and his lawyer failed to have the charges against him dropped, the reality of his situation began to hit hard. His denial collapsed as he began to face the fact that he would spend the next six or more years in gaol. To make matters worse for him, there were court hearings that he was not allowed to attend and did not even know about, at which further charges against him were being heard, and his sentence was being increased. He would be informed of this after the fact, and there was absolutely nothing he could do about it. He fell into a deep depression. The other inmates in the group offered compassion, sometimes in words but mostly in silence, as Harry began to deal with the acute pain and enormity of the loss he was now facing. For the first time in group, Nick expressed the beginnings of empathy. 'I've done a lot of gaol and I've never minded being in here,' he said. 'I know you're doing it hard, Harry. I think I would too if I had a lovely wife and family out there, like you. It must be real tough for you right now.'

Harry had taught Nick to care, and Nick began to care about himself. He began meditating in his cell, and expressed that he now accepted he had an entrenched problem with alcohol and criminal behaviour. Gradually, he became more responsive in group, saying that it was as if he was suddenly able to understand all the things I had been talking about all these years, for the first time. He expressed a desire not to return to his drinking-criminal lifestyle when he was released, to work on himself, and to see a neuro-psychologist for an alcohol-related brain-damage assessment as soon as he was able to organise it. At last Nick began revealing some insight into his behaviour. 'I'm getting it for the first time,' he'd say, 'now I can understand you, Jude.' He was quick to recognise how nothing had sunk in previously. Months later he was put onto the Work Release program and with a little help found himself a job — a real job! He went to work each day and came back 'home' to gaol at night, without drinking or going off the rails. Over the ensuing year he proved himself to be completely stable and reliable in his Work Release program, which was a gigantic step forward for him. His attendance at group revealed many positive changes were happening — he was attending AA meetings in gaol and his recovery was taking off at last. Nick's behavioural improvements and progress meant he was favourably considered for parole. The job gave him a sense of self-worth he had never experienced before, and the quiet support he received from Harry nurtured great change. Harry's caring made all the difference to Nick, and having a lost soul like Nick to care about, was a great awakener for Harry.

Working with people like Nick has shown me so often, how the caring and faith of just one person, either a counsellor or a friend, can enable a seemingly hopeless, very lost soul to turn themselves and their life around quite miraculously. All it takes is one person who genuinely cares! Being able to give in this way to our fellow human beings, in simple ways, can make a world of difference. The power of caring cannot be overestimated.

ॐ

At the age of twenty-six, Mohandas Gandhi reflected that he felt the worth of a nation depended on the character of its individuals, rather than the form of its institutions. Years later, as he led his movement towards Indian independence, he said, 'We must become the change we want to see.' Gandhi lived everything he espoused in proposing significant social and political change. His humility and deep adherence to a return to spiritual and human values in India, gave him, more than anything else, immense power to move, inspire and unite the disempowered masses of his beloved country. These very same attributes brought about his assassination.

As we change, our values change. The ego-personality values external things but the state of soul is value. For the soul, value exists without 'things' to attach it to. Soul-consciousness brings us into awareness of our intrinsic value. The ego-personality becomes powerfully caught up in the body and external things that it idealises. Focusing on people and things outside the self is how we lose our true sense of value. From the perspective of spirit, true value lies in integrity, honour, truth and soul-consciousness. From the perspective of ego-personality, value is in physical beauty, material success and worldly achievement. When people say they will 'sell their soul' to become rich, famous or important in materialistic terms, this is precisely what they do. The more ego-consciousness increases, the more devoid of values society becomes. There is a link between the experience of our own essential state of value and the expression and appreciation of values in the way we live. Our life is an expression of what is inside. Devoid of spiritual value, we live our lives according to the goals and ideals of a materialistic society. However, when we become aware of essential values and begin to express these in the way we live, we get in touch with our essential value. There is a resonant connection between the two.

Gandhi is a shining example of this. In the years prior to the awakening of his spiritual awareness, which occurred while he was in South Africa, he was an overly timid, rather spineless fellow. In a strange way, the challenges that confronted him as an Indian living under a racist regime proved to be the making of him. By the time he returned to India he had developed a spiritual discipline and a set of values based on purity, truth, love and the use of peaceful 'soul force'. He lived by these values, and he knew that the only way to get the British to leave India was to achieve this peacefully, through spiritual values and discipline. His ensuing twenty-year struggle tested everything he lived by and believed in, and was the real making of him, not only as an outstanding leader, but also as the greatest leader of the peace movement the world has known.

On 6 February 1916, in the Holy City of Benares, at an occasion described by Gandhi's biographer[19] as glittering with royalty, jewellery, formality and ringing with perfect British and educated Indian accents, Mohandas Gandhi, an invited speaker, wearing a short white dhoti and simple white shawl, entered the gathering. Forthright and direct, he made a characteristic extemporaneous speech that so affronted the attending maharajahs, Viceroy, Hindu leaders and the ruling class of India, he was asked to leave the Holy City the following morning. His speech addressed some core values regarding his motherland. First of all, he reminded everyone, he was required to make his speech in English, a language foreign to his country, rather than his native Hindi. Self-government and self-responsibility in India were his major issues, but he took the opportunity to remind the Indians who were present that their habit of spitting in public places and on trains (where people walked, sat and lay down) was inconsiderate and disgusting.

Gandhi was also greatly concerned with the capitalist grip the British had on India. Handicrafts and cottage industries had suffered under the auspices of the British Raj and Gandhi believed handloom weaving and hand spinning would do much to redress India's desperate poverty. Prior to British rule, every village in India was self-sufficient. Women wove their own cloth, a practice that kept them gainfully employed and brought dignity to their lives. However, the British exported Indian cotton to England, where it was milled in Lancashire and the cloth shipped back to India to be sold at a price most Indians could not afford. British exploitation struck at the heart of Indian society, devaluing and destroying the integrity of the Indian systems.

Gandhi knew that hand spinning could guarantee an income

for villagers during the seasons when work in the fields was scarce. A return of the spinning wheel would reinstate village industries and cut the country's requirement for British cloth. The cloth the villagers spin is known as 'khadi' and Gandhi's khadi movement would restore an ethos and a set of values to village life, which had been destroyed. Khadi was seen as an important part of Gandhi's contribution to raising consciousness in India. Wearing the simple, homespun cloth became the hallmark of the national movement. The spinning wheel became the symbol of brotherhood across the caste system and differing socio-economic backgrounds, reinforcing dignity, values, and bonding the people of India in a unique way.

Values were at the heart of Gandhi's inner journey and outer goals. He was a leader of humanity who confronted and dealt with his own inner demons before helping his followers, then the wider population, to deal with theirs. He helped the people of India face their own prejudices and attitudinal values where caste and religion divided them. He revealed to them that their unity and non-violent resistance would be more than a match for the British. Gandhi was a true leader who modelled values-based, integrated leadership. He would not allow the real issues of his society to be avoided, and kept them at the forefront of India's consciousness until she was free. For this he was assassinated.

Spiritual values are an expression of the soul, and as such, tend to be revealed in our attitude, consciousness and the way we live. *Simplicity* is a value that is practised and regarded very highly by those who lead a spiritual way of life. Buddha, Christ, Mohammed and Mohandas Gandhi exemplified this value. *Compassion* is a value which Buddha developed as the core of his teachings, whereas the value of *unconditional love* was central to the life and teachings of Christ. Each of these teachers revealed a very deep *humility* — the value and virtue that underpins greatness of soul. Their lives exemplified the values of *honesty, discernment, responsibility, peace, tolerance, respect, discipline, benevolence, caring* and *truth*. No matter whether Christ was among crowds of people, lepers, prostitutes, money lenders or his disciples, his life and all of his expression was infused with these same values. We remember Buddha more than two and a half thousand years after he lived, because his character and his life were an expression of truth and spiritual values.

To live according to these values of the soul is to live a 'valuable' life. Our character is defined by our values, and the development of a reformed character is the outcome of spiritual growth. Becoming aware of the inclusion of values in our way of life, and our relationships and interactions with others, is a primary focus of spiritual life.

The way of the modern world is based on a very different understanding of values. The greed machine has consumed the values that stabilised our existence and once made us feel that the world was a safe and nurturing place to roam. Economic rationalism, also known as the 'new capitalism', seems to have sealed its own fate, and ours with it. Without very substantial and far reaching values-based political, social, economic and financial reform, we stand to lose even the basic things, such as high quality education, health care and social systems, that contribute to the quality of life and the safe, comfortable standard of living we desire. Values-based training, leadership, systems and business will only result from new thinking that is the result of a values-based consciousness.

෴

Today in the West, evidence of a change in consciousness is apparent in the emergence of some ethical investments, business enterprises and organisations. In August 1996 a significant project took birth when a group of twenty educators met at UNICEF Headquarters in New York to discuss the needs of children. This meeting gave birth to *Living Values: An Educational Program*. From small beginnings, Living Values activities are now being carried out at over four thousand sites in sixty-seven countries[20] and a special program has been developed for refugees and children affected by war. Those behind the program realise that education is one of the most effective ways of reducing poverty, exclusion, ignorance, oppression and war. Learning to be and to live together are essential if the door to a culture of peace is to be opened. Described as 'The Quiet Revolution', the Living Values Program has been greeted with keen acceptance all over the world. The Living Values series of books won the 2002 Teachers' Choice of the Year Award in the USA. Diane Tillman, a Licensed Educational Psychologist from California, is the primary author of the LVEP materials.[21]

In 1999 Diane was invited into the jungles of Thailand to teach Living Values to teachers in the Karen Tribe, a group of 100,000 Burmese refugees who, since the revolution in 1988, have fled across the border to Thailand. Living in relatively inaccessible mountain villages that they have built themselves, these people carry the wounds of war, death, violence, upheaval and, of course, exclusion from their own country. The camp Diane was invited to had eleven thousand occupants then (it now has many more). Thirty-five refugee teachers participated in the initial training. Some of them had to walk for two and a half hours to attend each morning.

Children affected by war have been exposed to events that no adult, much less a child, should experience. The time spent in chaos and trauma deeply affects children and interferes with the acquisition of healthy intrapersonal and interpersonal functioning and skills.[22] As well as enabling children to explore values in all areas of their lives and learn positive skills in communication and conflict resolution, the program is designed to allow feelings of loss, grief and anger to be expressed in a safe, validating atmosphere.

During the training, participants were divided in two groups to participate in sessions on war and loss, in which they were encouraged to express their experiences through drawings and words. A peace puppet was passed around, to help some teachers who had earlier chosen not to speak, to share their stories. These sessions were extremely intense, but it was critical for the Karen teachers to experience their own reactions to these exercises, so as to develop understanding and faith in the process they would be initiating with their young charges. Finally, songs about peace and love were shared by both trainers and refugees.

Rachel Flower, the organiser and a co-trainer, visited the camp several times throughout the year to do follow-up work with the teachers and monitor theirs and the students' progress. The following year Diane and Rachel returned to the jungle to facilitate a second training and follow-up with the thirty-five trainees in the first group. (The second group of trainees had twenty-four teachers, as well as nine of the previous group who were training to be trainers.)

In a follow-up with the first group of trainees, all reported positive changes in their students. Apparently, the children expressed a great deal of interest in the Living Values lessons, revealing increasing levels of participation and expression. Some comments from the teachers were:

'The students now dare to speak'

'They share their pictures now, before they would just be quiet'

'Before when a camp leader would come to the class they would be quiet, now they not only dare to speak, they ask questions.'

The children in the camps were displaying encouraging behavioural changes; they were more playful, respectful, loving and friendly towards their peers and teachers. They were also trying harder with schoolwork and were reportedly 'less sad'. Fighting among the children had mostly ceased and they were openly observed to be teaching one another conflict resolution skills. As a result of the training, villagers too, initiated their own monthly meetings to share experiences and co-operate in problem solving.

Four training sessions have now taken place in the Karen camps along with a great deal of follow-up work and more are planned. The Living Values Education Program has been so successful that Karen Tribe teachers have now qualified as trainers and are conducting training sessions themselves.

ৡৡৡ

The ideal of a so-called value-free society comes at a price, and as many people are discovering, the price is costing us our humanity. When one set of values is removed another automatically takes its place, and in this case the removal of spiritual values from society has given way to values based on materialism, so the ideal of a value-free society has not, and never will be, a reality. Our values not only determine the physical, psychological and spiritual well-being of our civilisation, they also determine the state of our physical universe. It is not possible for a societal value to be adopted or lost, without this loss being mirrored in some way in the natural environment. For instance, loss of the spiritual value of *balance* has resulted in extremes of imbalance in human nature, a condition which is echoed in nature itself. For example, in disturbed weather patterns, an escalation in earthquakes, droughts, floods and other natural disasters causing environment imbalance. *Balance*, like all values, affects our inner lives as well as the environmental setting. Like Buddha and many living by ancient and tribal traditions, the

Greek philosophers valued and emphasised moderation, balance and restraint within the personal code of conduct, as part of their 'steady state' philosophy. If we want nature to come into balance and harmony, then we have to reinstate balance and harmony in ourselves first. Spiritual values are our key to creating a better world.

As the balance of power on the world stage becomes an issue of significant international concern the memory of the holocaust is a reminder that power is a vital issue when values disintegrate. A society which divests itself of values is like a vessel adrift at sea. Values are related to our conscience, which steers us through life and keeps us on a steady course, especially when confusion reigns. Values are our safe harbour in a social environment that has abandoned its compass points. When we let go of our spiritual values, we let go of everything.

The person who conquers his or her own base, ego-conscious nature, thus attaining complete spiritual power and sovereignty over the self, may then, and only then, have the power to rule the world. This is the natural law. A person or nation using any other means, including nuclear force, will never succeed in dominating the world, for it is the law of spirituality that none can take over the world through the use of physical force.

As the natural laws dictate and Mohandas Gandhi understood, with the armour of spirituality, and armed with the values of fearlessness, truth, love and non-violence — only then can we truly conquer the world!

chapter fifteen

SIMPLICITY

Simplicity is the art of being. As we become increasingly free of the ego-personality, complex life situations that may have once pulled us no longer hold any attraction. The desire for possessions and acquisition is reversed. Over time, our lifestyle becomes simple and we feel a pull to simplicity in all we do. Simplicity is a hallmark of the person who is moving along the spiritual path, of the soul who is becoming free.

Siddhartha, son of the Brahmin, knows how to soundlessly speak the om, breathe it into himself with all his soul. The exquisitely drawn character of Siddhartha in Herman Hesse's classic tale[23] possesses great depth of spirit, grace, clarity of intellect, and is loved by all. Yet, for all his attributes of physical beauty, good breeding, princely comfort and *sadhana* (spiritual effort), Siddhartha is not happy. He does not know joy. Renouncing his family and home, he wanders as a samana (a renunciate, one who seeks to be completely free from ego) for many years, developing in himself a profound simplicity. Upon meeting the revered Gautama Buddha in the forest and listening to the profound teachings he has to share, Siddhartha realises that following even the greatest of human teachers cannot deliver him from ego. He must become his own teacher, he must find his own way and deliver himself.

Embracing everything he has hitherto renounced, he explores his opposite polarities with 'the child people', his term for society. The beautiful courtesan, Kamala, whom he meets when entering a village, asks Siddhartha what a simple samana such as he can do. 'I can think, I can fast, and I can wait,' he replies. His

145

liaison with Kamala leads him to explore relationship with a woman and the finer arts of tantric lovemaking. In keeping with Kamala's values, he immerses himself totally in the world of business, wealth, material comfort, success and sensual pleasures. Eventually, having pursued sensual gratification with Kamala, he is confronted by the resulting hollowness of his existence. He realises they cannot experience true love for one another this way, and he knows he has forgotten how to think, to fast, and to wait.

Siddhartha has lost his simplicity, and knows he must return to a renunciate lifestyle to reconnect with his spirituality. While he is living by the river with the humble ferryman who is the embodiment of simplicity, wisdom and a soul nearing perfection, Siddhartha's life lessons bring him full-cycle to humility. He must come to know and experience the deep suffering of attachment, and the excesses of the physical, sensual and material, to truly understand and value the freedom and sweetness of simplicity and ultimately, egolessness.

Simplicity is the art of just being. Even the finest, most subtle threads of attachment become a veil which obscure the deep bliss and joy within. However, it is not necessary to live as a *samana* in the forest and to renounce all the trappings of a twenty-first century existence in order to experience simplicity. Renunciation does not mean living in austerity, but rather, renouncing ego-identification with possessions. For instance, we need a car, a home, clothes, and numerous other 'things' to maintain our existence at the physical level. If the clothing absolutely has to bear a Giorgio Armani label, then the ego identity is involved. In other words, there is attachment. When we lose connection with our spiritual value, we place this value on outer things, then become dependent on those things to feel good about ourselves.

Every decade of a person's life adds many layers to the personality and the complexities he or she adopts that continue to obscure and sever us from our essence. The process is subtle and continuously erosive.

Renunciation involves an attitude of detachment from material possessions. Mohandas Gandhi set an example of renunciation and poverty by possessing only one set of clothes — a short dhoti, a pair of sandals, plus a shirt and a shawl for the cold weather. The Buddha and Christ also made themselves examples of renunciation and simplicity, as have many others who have experienced a spiritual awakening and turned to the spiritual path. Leading the life of an ascetic for its own sake does not occasion spiritual growth any more than does living in a palace with priceless, sacred possessions. Maintaining a detached attitude from possessions is what is important.

A spiritual life involves the extraordinarily difficult art of balance. The spiritual path teaches us to avoid extremes of behaviour, to live simply, to be mindful of balance — to be moderate in all we do, and not allow ourselves to become too tired, to work too hard, to become over-involved or under-involved in what we do. By learning equanimity in all things — for example, in success and failure, praise and defamation, good fortune and adversity — a centred soul may live a life of balance and equanimity, rather than extremes. This too, is simplicity.

Inner peace and contentment arise from balance. A soul who is being pulled between the pairs of opposites in the personality experiences no peace and no happiness. The complete soul exists in a state of perfect balance and expresses this inner balance in all things. Inner calm leads to outer calm. The soul's inner environment will influence the outer environment and atmosphere. The more aligned with our spirituality we become, the more this will be reflected in a clean, open and harmonious environment. It will be a statement of simplicity. Creation of work and home environments will reveal a clear, welcoming, organised and pleasant space, filled with good vibrations instead of clutter and junk.

Material clutter is a sign of mental clutter. The home or work environment is a mirror of our inner environment. Inner work clears out mental and emotional clutter, creating a feeling of inner space. Inner spaciousness produces feelings of freedom and lightness, and as we clean out our inner space, our personal physical environment will become a reflection of this. The soul is the source of simplicity. Spaciousness within creates a reflection in many expressions. Simplicity of being is evident not only in the way we live but becomes very apparent in lifestyle, physical appearance, thoughts, communication style, interactions, relationships and our way of being in the world.

An individual who possesses simplicity will do one thing at a time and be completely focused on that one thing. After many years of observing very experienced yogis in everyday situations, it is apparent that when they eat, they focus entirely on eating. They do not read the paper or have a meeting while they are eating. When they have a cup of tea, they stop what they are doing and just focus on drinking the tea. When they read, they create the space to just read. When they have a meeting they give their entire attention to the meeting until it finishes. The moment the meeting is over, their thoughts have also left the meeting. When going for a walk, it is a walk and a time to commune with nature. They are completely focused in the present, one thing at a time. When they sleep, they sleep well and need several hours less sleep than the average person.

The mind of a yogi is still, silent and stable. There is no excess thought. They do not allow their mind to worry about anything, nor their thoughts to become anxious or distracted. While they can and do achieve a great deal in the course of a day's activities, they would never say they are busy. Because their mind is uncluttered, they think a minimum of thoughts, and only those that are necessary. They are always available, because with nothing on their mind, they can give themselves completely to the moment and task at hand. At the inner and outer level, they accomplish a great deal with ease. This is simplicity. The mind is an obedient servant. It does not dwell on the past nor the future and there is no inner conflict. All tasks are given total attention until they are finished. The practised yogi completes everything and moves into the next activity freely. In this way, unfinished business does not accumulate, or prevent full attention on the present.

When being busy is a perpetual state of being, energy is fast so there is disconnection from the self and over connection with the environment. The person who 'must' keep busy and habitually over commits themselves either with work, social life or other things, will spend a lot of time and valuable energy avoiding themselves and their feelings. They frequently speak of 'how busy' they are — the mantra of the twenty-first century — and unnecessarily complicate their lives. The ability to concentrate and focus without extraneous thought reveals a slow, accurate intellect and simplicity of thinking. The intellect disciplined by meditation exercises absolute control over the mind ensuring that this is the case. Simplicity is freedom.

The mind that races — thoughts and words tumbling out, interrupting others habitually in conversation, unable to listen or wait until others can complete what they are saying, wanting fast answers and instant information — is a mind out of control. Energy vibrating erratically creates inner chaos, frequently reflected in minor, or perhaps even major health problems. 'But I don't have time to meditate!' is the catch phrase of the chaotic ego-personality. The goals and conditioning of the material world lead us away from self-discovery, they lead us away from ourselves. Reliance on 'things' outside the self leads to reinforcement of the false self and the emptiness this brings.

Worrying about anything which has or has not happened is self-destructive. Reducing life's problems into small, manageable proportions enables us to deal with things one at a time, without giving up our power and confidence. Negative and critical thoughts undermine the soul, whereas positive, constructive thinking empowers us. Simplifying things at the level of thought means simplifying life.

When the mind is centred, still and silent, I act and respond from the solid core of myself. There is no scattering of energy, words, thought or action. Economy is a sign of simplicity. When I am economical with my thoughts, my words are an expression of soul and are filled with meaning and truth. When I am anchored in my true self, relationships and interactions become easy and simple. The clarity and distinction between I and Thou is not transgressed, for my boundaries are clear.

While working in Vietnam I was taken to visit a colleague's property in the countryside just outside Ho Chi Minh City. The property consisted of an orchard and an old, rather quaint, ramshackle house. The owners lived in the city and had asked a Buddhist nun to stay in the house and look after it for them. There was no telephone at the house. Inside, a worn black and white marble floor greeted us as we entered and just a few pieces of rustic furniture. Otherwise it was bare, dark and reminiscent of a Buddhist temple, with a very large altar upon which incense was burning. Thin shafts of sunlight filtered through the shuttered windows. The nun spoke no English and was dressed in characteristic brown cloth that was very worn. When we entered she asked us to light some incense, which we placed on the altar. After a brief tour we went outside into the bright, sunlit orchard, where I noticed a small vegetable garden and the nun's clothes hanging out to dry. They were little more than threadbare rags, clearly she was very poor. Moving into the overgrown gardens we found a shaded area with table and seats, to sit and talk. The nun produced boiled water in thermos flasks which had seen much better days. These were placed hospitably before us.

When it came time to leave the nun returned to say goodbye to us. I observed her gentle demeanour, her hands and fingernails that worked the earth to grow her own food. I asked how she spent her time here, all alone, and what her spiritual practice meant to her. My friend acted as translator. 'She says she spends all of her time meditating and praying for the spiritual upliftment of our country. This is all, this is her whole life.' Her round face was soft and her liquid brown eyes were large pools of light. A radiant, compassionate being was shining through those eyes. Gazing into them I felt the warmth of her love and silence. I wanted to give her something, to let her know that I felt a connection with her. Words were not necessary, I could see and feel the unmistakable sign of recognition. Deep inside, I was touched by her simplicity. Such moments pass in the flicker of an eye, yet this kind of contact is precious and special to me, and never forgotten.

Most of what I observed in Vietnam moved me. I saw a people struggling to put the past behind them, to move forward in peace and co-operation. I watched the way they flowed and moved along their crowded roads. Very rarely did anyone stop. Their system is to keep flowing and to go around whatever might be in the way. Crossing the road on foot is an interesting exercise in faith, as the traffic never stops. It is all done through eye contact with the riders and drivers, who simply ride around pedestrians as they cross. It took a little while to get the hang of it. Given the volume of traffic and the huge numbers of people, this was remarkable. Not once did I witness a trace of irritation, anger or violence. The ancient traditions and practices of Asia are grounded in Buddhism and Taoism, which appear to have enabled the people to accept and accommodate the trauma of war and political upheaval, with minimum disruption to their lives — like the 'zen' of managing crisis and change.

The natural wisdom of the soul is rooted in humility and inner vision. The ferryman who was Siddhartha's mentor rarely spoke, but he listened and observed from the depth of his soul. It is not clever words or the sound of one's voice that brings enlightenment to others, it is the soul's deep silence and wisdom of experience imparted in every action and expression. Knowledge for the sake of being clever does not enable the soul to make spiritual progress, instead it feeds the ego identity and supports the inflation of the false self. When a teacher is very articulate and clever with words, even spiritual information may be used to glorify the self rather than benefit others. When truth becomes contaminated by ego or falsehood, happiness disappears.

In their simplicity of being, children use their spirituality creatively and spontaneously to play and to grow. As adults, we express these qualities fully as we develop spiritually. Herman Hesse's Siddhartha took leave of his Brahmin household to experience, learn and taste the complexity of existence in order to attain and value simplicity. Our journey to spiritual completion means embracing and integrating our complex and serious 'adult nature', as we return to our natural simplicity, playfulness, and child-like joy and innocence — through the wisdom and experience of maturity.

chapter sixteen

PEACE

The original state of the soul is peace. When the soul becomes disconnected from itself and from its peace, slipping into a consciousness in which violence becomes possible, the world, too, becomes a place where violence becomes possible. When the soul brings violence into action, the world becomes a place of violence, and our original state of peace disappears. As is the soul, so is the world.

Returning to soul-consciousness brings the soul's natural state of peace into being once again, and as more and more souls change consciousness, the world becomes increasingly conscious of the need for peace, and of a deep desire to attain this state of being. Everyone wants peace. As we souls awaken spiritually and return to our natural consciousness and state of peace, we let go of fear and influence the world more powerfully than any weapon of violence or mass destruction. Peace is the weapon of love, truth and fearlessness.

༺๛༻

A cloud of white doves rises symbolically above the United Nations (UN) headquarters in New York. It is 1986, the United Nations International Year of Peace (IYP). White doves mark the launch of what promises to be an important year of consciousness-raising. NGOs (non-government organisations) are preparing their projects internationally. Before the year ends, UN peace projects will have been taken up by numerous governments, school children, educational and religious institutions, private companies and people from all walks of life. President

Gorbachev will have convinced President Reagan to enter into a nuclear disarmament agreement.

The Brahma Kumaris sponsor the Million Minutes of Peace Appeal, an international project collecting donations of minutes of prayer, meditation and peaceful thoughts. During one month the organisation gathers almost a billion minutes of peace from around the globe. Walkers carry a peace flame around the world in an International Peace Walk. As the year comes to a close something unique has touched the consciousness of millions of people. It is the power of peace. When this power sweeps us up in its magic, it touches the very soul of humanity and reaches in to the core of our being, disarming the personality and its armour-like defences. When the heart energy opens, something unforgettable takes place, as it did in 1986 and again in 2000 in Sydney during the Olympic Games. The power of peace is within us all. When people experience this power, anything becomes possible.

Peace does not come from an external source, it is not legislated or negotiated. Peace cannot be controlled or shaped. Peace springs from a peaceful consciousness and it is this alone that creates a peaceful society. While anger, fear, resentment, hatred, jealousy or bitterness exist in our community, even at the level of thought, there cannot be peace. Peace is not an absence of violence, but is present where there is non-violence at the level of thought. Attacking the self with criticism and negativity is one of the most common forms of violence. To attack the self in this way means that sooner or later you will attack others. When verbal violence is directed at you from an external source the words can linger in your heart for months or longer, eroding your peace and self-esteem. It is amazing how contagious one person's peacelessness can become.

A popular saying goes, 'The price of freedom is eternal vigilance', a statement which reveals a complete lack of understanding of peace and is a contradiction in terms, as eternal vigilance suggests a constant looking over the shoulder, a taut wariness and watchfulness. These are hardly the kinds of experiences associated with freedom, yet they are the expressions of our world.

৵৽

The movement from individual peace to global peace is happening in silence, in the privacy of the soul. With each soul that awakens and begins to realise itself, the power of peace in our world grows. One by one, day by day, as more souls realise themselves, a change in consciousness is reinforced. It is happening peacefully everywhere. As more souls experience a shift in consciousness, the world consciousness also shifts. If world leaders want to create peace, they must bring about a change in their own consciousness and make themselves peaceful, because this is the only way any of us will achieve peace. Peace begins with me. When I take responsibility for changing my consciousness, another giant step towards world peace is taken. It is easy to attend a peace rally and make a public statement of support for non-violence through our physical presence, which is a valid and important means of expression, but it is another matter entirely to face our inner selves.

The personality possesses many dark corners and hidden, shadowy places in which the memories, traits and emotions that destroy our peace are stored. Without peace there is no happiness. Peace is the basis of a positive, balanced state of mind and inner well-being. Without inner peace we have nothing.

Whatever belongs to the past needs to be freed and let go. When I take responsibility for my part in unresolved situations and interactions from the past, I liberate myself from their disquieting hold on me. Even small threads of unfinished business will unconsciously distance me from the deep peace and contentment that is my true nature. Being at peace with myself is a great attainment, since the personality has an armoury of tactics to keep me in a state of distraction.

The soul-conscious state can be violated very easily by the personality. It is necessary to use the power of realisation and awareness that come with soul-consciousness to dismantle the emotional blocks and destructive behaviours that are carried in the layers of our personality. Inner peace is achieved through the practice of soul-consciousness with the willingness to examine, own and let go of negative processes and behaviours. There are no shortcuts to inner peace, this path requires determination and a strong commitment to self-change. Real peace and freedom come at a price, but the cost of remaining in old destructive patterns is ultimately much higher. Mohandas Gandhi could never have achieved what he did, without total commitment to self-change.

Peace is a state of vulnerability. The soul is completely and naturally vulnerable, but at the same time it is indestructible. The defensive ego creates behaviour that results in irritation, anger, revenge and confrontation between individuals, groups and nations. Without letting go of defence and making ourselves completely vulnerable, we cannot experience inner peace nor create an atmosphere of global peace. The most valuable assets we have are the qualities of just being a soul. It is soul-consciousness that enables the soul to be stable, unshakeable, compassionate, loving and detached, no matter what happens.

The value of peace is experienced in sharp contrast to the shattering experience of violence. In her studies on the impact of violence on our society, author Judith Lewis Herman[24] points out that as an innocent bystander witnessing violence, it is morally impossible not to take sides. It is seductive to take the side of the perpetrator, because all they ask is for our silence, that we do nothing. On the other hand, the victim requires that we share the burden of their pain, that we become engaged, take action, and resist the powerful temptation to 'see, hear and speak no evil.' When we value truth and non-violence, our conscience is engaged in upholding these values. One of the reasons Mohandas Gandhi was so deeply loved and respected, was that he committed himself to share the burden of the victim, and to see, hear and speak of the evil, openly and without compromise. First he had to face his own inner perpetrator, as must we all, in order to become peaceful and free.

FORGIVENESS AND PEACE
Mohandas Gandhi wrote:

We in India may in a moment realise that one hundred thousand Englishmen need not frighten three hundred million human beings. A definite forgiveness would mean a definite recognition of our strength. With enlightened forgiveness must come a mighty wave of strength in us.[25]

The connection between forgiveness and peace was one which Gandhi took to heart. His idea of an enlightened forgiveness creating a great strength in the people was a reminder of how peaceful Indians had been, historically, despite their country being invaded and looted scores of times. The Moghuls transported gold and precious jewels out of the country by the cart load during their invasions. The British too, looted much of what remained of India's wealth. Gandhi's philosophy of non-violent resistance, unity and 'soul force' was a very dignified response to the British invasion and a fitting reminder of a people whose dignity had, for a long time, placed them above recourse to violence. As leverage for independence, his peaceful weapon of satyagraha inspired three hundred million people and achieved its aim, exactly as he predicted. In response to outbreaks of violence among his fellow countrymen Gandhi fasted. So loved and respected was he, that he was able, through fasting, to bring the outbreaks of bloodshed to a halt.

While the British suppressed the aggression between Muslim and Hindu, Gandhi realised the only way to attain self-rule was through a peaceful India in which rich and poor, educated and illiterate, Hindu, Muslim, Sikh, and all castes and religions were united. He made himself an example of tolerance, forgiveness and brotherly love towards all — including the British.

On 15 August 1947, India was granted independence from Britain. Mohandas Gandhi fought the partition of India and Pakistan until he was forced to retreat, due to threats of fresh outbreaks of violence. On 26 January 1948, Indian Independence day was celebrated with thousands shouting slogans of unity and harmony in the streets, 'Hindu-Muslim, bhai-bhai (brother-brother).' Gandhi's residence became a pilgrimage place, but Gandhi was so perturbed and demoralised, he was unable to give a message for the people, to the BBC. Among the things that troubled him so deeply, were the differences between Nehru (India's new Prime Minister) and Vallabhbhai Patel, the Home Minister, both of whom he had worked with, for so long. Their differences threatened to undo everything Gandhi had worked for.

Biographer Yogesh Chadha, in *Rediscovering Gandhi*[26] relates how Gandhi shared his grave concerns with Louis Mountbatten, Viceroy of India. Before retiring on 29 January 1948, he shared more concerns with his granddaughter Manubhen about the mounting evidence of corruption in his Congress. Office and power were luring those who had worked with him for freedom, so hard and for so long. 'How can we look the world in the face?' a very disturbed, seventy-four year old Gandhi had confided to Manu, 'Where do I stand and what am I doing?'[27]

The following evening, weaving through the throng at his prayer meeting, Gandhi stopped as he neared the stage and bowed in the traditional manner of namaskar, bringing his hands together. At that moment his assassin fired at point-blank range.

Three bullets and a few moments later, Gandhi died. When Nehru arrived, he knelt beside the lifeless body and wept unrestrainedly. According to Chadha, Lord Mountbatten was informed and rushed to where Gandhi's body had been carried. Both Patel and Nehru were in the room when Mountbatten arrived. Instinctively, he drew the leaders aside and shared with them Gandhi's deep wish for them to resolve their differences. Nehru and Patel looked at one another, their gaze shifting to the shrouded body on the floor, then in silence they walked towards each other and embraced. Twenty-five years later, during an interview for a book, Mountbatten wept openly as he described entering Birla House that January afternoon and seeing Gandhi's body laid out on his straw pallet.[28]

Motivated by love and compassion, Gandhi not only moved the people of India, he moved the world. His experience suggests that without spiritual awareness, unity and non-violence are not possible. Gandhi lived his practice, he did not waste empty words. Through his spiritual commitment to brahmacharya, simplicity, unity and non-violence, he infused in his fellow countrymen an awesome hope and inspiration. They were swept up by the force of tolerance, forgiveness and love, as the power of satyagraha surged through India, uniting religious extremists and castes. No other peacemaker in history has had such a profound influence or revealed such a remarkable ability to lead, as Gandhi.

Amid the current world climate it is worth remembering what one soul was able to achieve in one lifetime without recourse to violence, threats, or military might. Peace is not beyond our reach, it is our original nature and our birthright. From the moment we begin to change our consciousness, we take an important step towards creating world peace. The right to peace is ours, the responsibility begins with each one of us. Like Gandhi, all we have to do is claim it.

chapter seventeen

INITIATION

Initiation is an informal rite of passage that a person making a firm spiritual commitment will, at some time, undergo. It involves 'dying alive': part of the personality has to be surrendered in a symbolic 'walk through fire'. The person's commitment is truly examined, their ego punctured. The vows are made from a place in us that is raw and exposed when we come before God stripped of complacency and false confidence. Initiation in the spiritual sense is never planned, nor does it take the form of a ritual celebration. It happens when we are vulnerable and seemingly unprepared. The crucifixion of Christ symbolises the initiation many souls experience when they come into relationship with God, leaving the old life and ascending to the next. After the 'death', love is poured into the bruised soul as the Beloved tenderly draws His treasured prize out of the darkness, into the light. Spiritual initiation tends to be realised retrospectively.

Tribal people honour and ritualise rites of passage such as the passing from girlhood into womanhood. Religious organisations too, recognise coming of age and commitment to the faith, with rituals such as bar mitzvah or confirmation. Tribal cultures idealise displays of courage and bravery through endurance of physical pain and challenge, as tribal elders initiate their young. Afterwards, the young adolescent is no longer a child. He has passed into manhood and the adult world of responsibility and choice. He has experienced suffering and relinquished a part of himself that was soft, childlike, needy and innocent, in exchange for strength and independence. One aspect of this phenomenon is clear — spiritual initiation is a breaking away from childhood in order to grow. It comes as soon as we are ready, and is a powerful 'make or break' experience, often stripping away many layers of ego at a single stroke. Rites of passage mark our lives in significant ways. The initiation I was about to undergo would indelibly mark mine.

Two years after my initial contact with the Brahma Kumaris, I boarded a flight bound for India — my first trip to the headquarters of the organisation in Rajasthan. From Los Angeles, Delhi is halfway around the world. It seemed miraculous that in two years so many things about me had changed, although naturally and gradually. I had not made enormous efforts to change, I just meditated and somehow the transformation was gently yet assuredly in motion. The 'honeymoon' was still in full swing and I felt that every footstep I took was divinely guided.

At the end of a very long and arduous flight the smell of the subcontinent filled the plane, although we were still miles above it. At four o'clock in the morning we were dumped on the tarmac in Delhi. It was the Indian spring of 1986. Hot asphalt, heat, pollution and the unmistakable smell of India invaded our senses, greeting us as we climbed out of the plane. The baggage handlers were either asleep or on strike, and our baggage was laid out near the plane. After a long walk dragging suitcases, we queued up in an even hotter corrugated iron shed, which served as the Delhi International Terminal. The immigration officers were not on duty, so we waited in line for them to arrive. In that airless oven my spirits were taking a decided turn for the worse, when suddenly something changed. A charge of energy began in my gut, rising and coursing through my body in a blissful wave of release. Excitement and what felt unmistakably like nostalgia surged through me. All I could think was, 'I'm home!'

My first visit to India was an initiation in every way and, except for craving a cigarette, one I embraced with the joy and innocence of a child. I was not alone, there was an unmistakably childlike exuberance and spontaneity in those around me. An overnight train journey on the Ashram Express took us from Delhi into Rajasthan, eventually snaking alongside the foothills of the Aravali mountain range, where we alighted into the platform culture of Abu Road Station. Everything and everyone around me held an extraordinary fascination. Our destination was Mount Abu, a hill station hidden high above the world, in the cool heights of the Aravali range, where many new people would enter my life. Madhuban (meaning forest of honey), the name of the BK headquarters, seemed very remote from the world, erasing all consciousness of time. The atmosphere on the mountain top was carefree and intoxicating.

Mount Abu hill station nestles around the shores of Nakki Lake, which fills the crater of an extinct volcano. Its main bazaar is a quaint array of shops selling saris, Kashmir shawls, jewellery, artefacts, clothing and food. It was bustling with Indian holiday-makers. Kashmiri Shikara (boat) rides on the lake offered a new experience in bliss, with just the sound of lapping water and the gentle movement of the boat being rowed by an oarsman at the stern. Hours before the dawn, under a canopy of brilliant stars, we moved through the darkness, all in white, to gather in meditation — the pure atmosphere infused with silence. In the stillness this felt like a gathering of angels.

Absorbing the unique culture of Madhuban for a whole month, I forgot the world, my life, my problems and even the cast of characters that populated my existence. Although I was blithely unaware of it, this month would provide the foundation of a major turning point, the repercussions of which I would feel intensely during the coming year, a year that would prove to be my true initiation to the spiritual life.

Up until now, I had the feeling of being carried with the current. I had not sensed I was guiding myself, making choices or even making decisions. If anything, I had been extremely reserved, going with the flow and observing all that was happening. All the events of the past two years snapped into shape and took on a deeper meaning and purpose. Madhuban is a place in which the soul may come very close to the Supreme Soul, this is part of its specialness. It is like no other place. So infused is the atmosphere with the power and vibration of God, many think they have found Heaven on Earth. For me, it was a personal encounter charged with intimacy and super-sensuous joy, day in and day out. So much so, that within days of my arrival I had fallen in love with this Soul, this God, unreservedly. Never in my wildest imaginings had I conceived an experience such as this would be possible! The month drew to a close, and in a heightened state of being, I descended the mountain, homeward bound.

Does love really change us? The India that awaited was different now, or was I different? The vibration at the bottom of the mountain was an unwelcome entry into another reality, one that no longer held any fascination, with an energy that now seemed abrasive and dirty. By the time we walked along Abu Road Station platform I knew I had already lost something and I felt the loss acutely. The pristine spiritual atmosphere of Madhuban was on top of that mountain and I was here, back in the Iron-Aged world in a country where 'Iron Age' takes on a whole new meaning. The train trip back to Delhi reinforced the deep sense of loss I was experiencing. I shared a sleeping compartment with five other passengers who had reserved seats, three of whom were Hindu. The Indians had enough luggage to push all of us out of the compartment. Once we were seated a few more found their way in and shoved and pushed until miraculously, they were all seated. One of them lit a cigarette, the smell was appalling!

Eventually a guard came and threw the extras out, so that we were able to pull out our bunks. The train windows were left wide open in the heat. The next morning one of my fellow travellers stuck her head over the top bunk to say 'good morning,' in a perfect British accent. She was wearing a sleeping mask which she then removed. Her face was black, leaving white oval shapes around her eyes. Our crisp white clothes were also now black. The symbolic nature of this did not escape me, but I was not prepared for re-entry into the great, crowded, dirty, noisy metropolis of Delhi. I was trying desperately to cling to the memory and the experience of Mount Abu.

All too soon I was in London, then New York. By the time the Statue of Liberty greeted me, I had an intuitive feeling about what lay ahead. While I was in India something had shifted, something had irrevocably changed. A definite conviction about my spirituality, purpose and relationship with God had taken the place of reservations and question marks. In my heart I had consolidated a deep commitment to live in a binding relationship with this Soul, in the highest tradition of brahmacharya (purity in thought, word and deed). Celibacy is a fundamental aspect of brahmacharya, although the practice embraces much more than abstinence, and represents a deep spiritual commitment. I do not make commitments lightly.

By the time I returned from India, I had been observing the practice of brahmacharya for almost two years. Brahmacharya is among a group of spiritual practices which are based on the highest principles of spirituality, principles that are carefully observed by those who feel ready to make a lasting commitment to the spiritual path, surrendering themselves to God completely in mind, body and spirit. When I had known the BKs for just three months, I did not know much about what they were doing, and none of them had mentioned the subject of brahmacharya to me. They obviously were celibate, and if I thought this was odd, I did not ask them about it. How the notion of me adopting this practice popped into my head is curious. Celibacy was not something I ever thought about, but in my state of newly awakened curiosity it seemed as if I was being guided into things

I had never thought about.

As my first experimental month of brahmacharya concluded I knew that I felt different, and I liked the 'difference'. Somehow, I felt much lighter. During my meditation that marked the end of that month, in a very subtle state I had the experience of being removed from the world and objectively seeing the subtle web of games and expectations that underlie human interaction at this level. I saw clearly how the power of sexual attraction and relationship drowns the subtlety of the spiritual experience, how it obliterates the connection with God, and how it contaminated my self-esteem. I was aware of an increase in my respect for others, and seeing myself and others in a more spiritual way felt surprisingly good. This was quite a shift for me — brahmacharya was beginning to make sense.

After three months had elapsed I had gained a whole new perspective on social and sexual values, and the mixed messages of society that I had long taken for granted. With this awareness came a new sense of freedom and wholeness — and of betrayal. I was questioning and thinking more deeply about social values than I ever had. Celibacy was not only becoming very attractive, but a brilliant way of rebelling against the values of a society which, I now felt, had really let me down. A totally new sense of empowerment and confidence took birth in my awareness. My commitment to brahmacharya seemed to open up a whole new realm of exciting possibilities. I was hooked.

One of my friends happened to be a sex therapist, and was a strong proponent for unrestrained sexual expression in all human beings. I was curious as to how she would receive my new, enlightened perspectives on a subject she clearly considered herself to be the expert in. Listening in barely disguised horror, she raised herself to her full height, drew a deep breath, and said, 'Judith, I would never recommend celibacy to any of my clients, or my friends!' Her response was rather gratifying, my new rebellion was working!

To be cured of all the diseases of the ego takes time, and being a brahmachary was elevating my level of self-awareness, and doing powerful groundwork for my healing. If I had arrived in Madhuban harbouring doubts about BK, before leaving I knew beyond any doubt at all, that I belonged to God and that God belonged to me. The kind of passion I was experiencing for this Soul, a passion beyond the senses, was very strange.

As the plane touched down in New York I was wondering how I might explain all that had happened in India to Jack, a friend who was eagerly awaiting my arrival. Jack's life had taken some unexpected twists and turns over the past year or two, and the changes both of us had negotiated steered us into a much greater level of intimacy. I was really looking forward to seeing him again. The Indian experience left me open and vulnerable, but otherwise unprepared for what was coming next. His joy at seeing me was unrestrained. The bond of several years of friendship had created a very special and safe feeling for us both. But as our drama was to dictate, in those first warming moments of seeing and greeting someone who is at once familiar and comforting, the absolutely unexpected phenomena of love hit us like a meteor. Given the new forces that had been gathering spiritually in my life over the past two years, culminating with my experience in India, the situation was not without irony.

For a start, the timing was terrible. Furthermore, how to deal with what was happening? The days passed and I felt more and more torn between my relationship with God, and fully entering a relationship with a human being — one that potentially offered so much. I was being forced to make a choice between my old life and a new one that had barely begun. Part of me was still tethered to my old dreams about 'perfect love fulfilled', and as much as I might try to deny that part of myself, it was speaking to me with an urgent voice. Jack was very supportive of my spiritual explorations from the moment I shared them with him, and had experimented with meditation in his own way. Now he asked eagerly whether I 'had done my spiritual thing yet', entreating me to move to New York and live with him, to let him support me while I explored my creative pursuits. The part of me that was drawn to this kind of love and closeness began to feel the pain of making a life choice that, either way, would have far reaching consequences.

India's magic was more distant now. Thus began the first real test of my commitment to God, to brahmacharya, and to the spiritual life. At times I would have preferred to slip quietly away from the BKs, as I was feeling uncomfortably invaded and compromised. Somehow, as I began wanting my privacy with Jack, they began to feel omnipresent. They were keen to engage my professional expertise for a service project in New York that would involve me spending some time in Manhattan at various intervals throughout the year. I felt very doubtful about committing myself for a number of reasons, but finally agreed despite all. When Jack and I parted at the airport, an uncertainty had crept between us, and I felt responsible. I didn't want to hurt him or compromise our relationship, and here I was doing both. A part of me did not want to let him go. After boarding my flight, I cried all the way to Los Angeles. The 'honeymoon' that had swept me up in a wave of divine bliss for the past two years was most definitely over.

The BK project proved to be extremely time consuming. A very good friend from LA got involved in it with me, and eventually another person joined us. Our job was to produce a concert and grand finale event for the conclusion of the International Year of Peace project in a venue that held ten thousand people. My mandate was that the event was to cost the BKs nothing, which meant I also had to raise money to cover the production costs. For an event that size in New York, this was a lot more than small change. It was a perilous position for me, but I decided to put my faith in God that all would be taken care of.

We worked day and night for almost nine months,

approaching an endless list of artistes, celebrities, musicians, public figures and a large number of organisations, to put a program together. Charitable events such as this involve a vast amount of organising on all levels, and things do not fall into place until the eleventh hour because most people are not willing to commit to appear without a fee until the last minute. One of the producers working with me gave us plenty of warning that nerves of steel would be required until the very last minute. 'But', he added, 'things always fall into place!'

The money we needed to cover our production budget did not fall from Heaven, and by the time the production team and I left for New York we had still not raised anywhere near the amount required. We arrived in New York exhausted from months of overwork to face the wrath of certain members of the organisation over the financial issue. If I had fallen short in my undertaking to the BKs, it was not for want of trying. I had done my best and could do no more. Shortly after a party of BKs arrived from overseas, I was taken to task again, this time over the planning of the program. It was made very clear to me that these people did not like anything I had planned for the event. They said they intended to take over and reorganise it themselves, based on a very simple and small program they had done in another country. In short, I was asked to step down and leave them to it — I was devastated.

What my team had planned was on quite a large scale and as seasoned professionals, we knew it would work. The battles that were now derailing our valuable production period had to be resolved quickly, leaving me no option but to step down and leave the others on my team to try to see it through. Some situations demand a symbolic spilling of blood, and in this instance the blood had to be mine.

A very strong ethic about always finishing what I start had been deeply instilled into me throughout my childhood and adolescence. To be prevented from doing the staging and seeing the show through to its conclusion was a heartbreaking wrench.

As I had discovered earlier in life that physical motion was a palliative, I walked the bustling streets of Manhattan and eventually found myself in Central Park, gravitating towards Strawberry Fields — John Lennon's memorial. The beautifully manicured English lawns of soft, emerald green grass offered me solace and a quiet place to feel the deep pain and betrayal of what was happening. Sitting by the large black and white mosaic of 'Imagine', my tears could have filled an ocean, but I could not make sense of anything. The feeling that I had been made a pariah was compounding deep feelings of loss and humiliation. I decided the best thing for me to do was confer with my colleagues then leave New York as soon as possible. After buying a packet of cigarettes and walking around Central Park for many hours I headed back, arriving at my hotel after eleven in the evening. I had eaten nothing all day and felt emotionally drained.

The door to my room was ajar and the LA team were sprawled on beds and chairs. I stood in the doorway feeling like a ghost, as they stared at me. Eventually one of them broke the silence. 'I've been calling you since ten this morning, you've been gone all day! Yoko Ono's lawyer called first thing, he says she wants to give permission for the video tribute we've done to go ahead, but he wanted it in his office ASAP this morning. Now the whole day's gone. Judi, what is going on and where the hell have you been? I know something is going on but no one will tell us anything!

'I've been thrown out, so has John Lennon, they don't want anything we've planned. I told them it won't work, it's too late to change things now. I can't believe no one has told you! This morning I was fired. I've just come back to talk to you about it. I think I should pack my things and leave first thing.' A stunned silence.

'You can't leave! We're only here because of you, this is your show!'

We talked well into the night and resolved between us that I should stay, while they continued to work on the show with the others and try to make the best of it. I was grateful for their dignity and integrity. When I finally sat down quietly to meditate, all I could see and feel were lightning bolts streaking across the room, right into my forehead.

The show went on more or less as originally planned and was a memorable event. As the evening concluded, a young woman took the stage sitting at a large, shiny black concert grand, and began singing the signature song she had written which had launched the project across America and been played countless times across the world. The rise and fall of her voice, resonant with feeling, rang out through the vast, vaulted cathedral. The atmosphere was alive with magic. Bringing the evening to a close, thousands of people moved towards the stage to light candles from a flame that had been walked around the earth for peace. The house lights were dimmed as people left in silence, like fireflies, scattering candle light into the streets and the warm Manhattan evening. Savouring the final scenes and the end of my ordeal, I left the venue alone. My escape was intercepted by one of my 'adversaries' who found me in the dim light, and eyes shining, threw her arms around me saying, 'It was your show, and it was absolutely wonderful!' The words were meaningless. I walked back to my hotel through the city streets, feeling a numb emptiness, realising I could not remember anything of the concert, except the very end of it.

Early the next morning I went to the United Nations building to say goodbye to one of the BK heads. I had felt her support through the entire ordeal and had been impressed by her detachment, and superior ability to manage crises. As I left the office we were in, another head of the organisation was sitting alone in an alcove off the hallway. Her face turned towards me and her eyes looked into mine. In a silent outpouring of compassion and love, she held out her hand to me. Wordlessly, I took it. Looking into her eyes the profound loss I was feeling seemed to envelop my heart, all I wanted to do was fall into her arms and weep. Both of these remarkable women had affected me deeply. With that, I left my short but memorable association with the Brahma Kumaris.

Jack dropped me off at the airport. 'You know what you need to do?' he said, 'you need to get angry. You need to get really angry!' I had no reply. After a while he asked me very gently, for the last time, 'Have you done your spiritual thing yet? Are you ready for a relationship?' I reached for his hand and squeezed it.

'I've made this so difficult, I'm so sorry Jack.' We hugged then parted in silence. I walked away feeling very sad, and when I eventually looked back he was driving away. The commitment I had made to be brahmacharya remained unbroken, but it felt like hauling in an empty net at the end of a month's fishing. As I walked away from Jack I knew how much I had changed.

The comfort of being alone with my feelings was all I had. My life had come to a sudden standstill after so much activity, and the future was a complete blank. Being in overdrive for so long had damaged my resilience, while an identity crisis loomed over me like a black cloud. My dalliance in New York had excised multiple layers of ego and I had no idea who I was any more, nor did I really care. I went back to work deciding to treat myself very gently.

Although I had no contact whatsoever with the BKs, my lifestyle remained as it had been. I continued meditating for many hours each day, it was a part of me now, but a large void had formed and I felt as if it was filled with sadness and anger. One evening in meditation the gentle, familiar voice spoke to me again, 'Will you not claim your inheritance from me, just because of one or two people?' The Psychologist was back! It was a simple enough question. I had to ask myself, did those few people represent the entire organisation? Did they represent God? The answer was obviously no, not now anyway, but somehow I had been seeing it differently. Who was my core relationship with, those people or God? Clearly, it was with God. What was the organisation anyway? It was a group of separate individuals who shared a common recognition of God, a common lifestyle and belief system, but who also held widely differing perspectives and opinions on most other matters. I still felt like a pariah — but God seemed to be entreating me to rise above all of that!

I had clarity, but the idea of returning to the meditation centre brought up so much pain I could hardly bear to think about it. But then, why should I give everything away just because of one or two people? It did not make sense! Perhaps this was one of those situations where I had to get back on the horse after being thrown or lose my confidence forever. I decided to get back on the horse.

Summoning all of my resources, I took myself to the centre for 6am meditation and class, and sat close to the door. The instant class was finished I left, thereby avoiding any contact or questions. After a week or so of this I had a call from Mary. When I answered the phone she said immediately, 'I just want to say ... when you walked back into class the other morning ... I'll never forget the feeling, I wanted to jump up and cheer!' She rang off.

Somewhere, deep in my soul, I knew I could never go back to the world I had come from. But was I really ready to give up my old nature? Surrender now felt like cold, razor-sharp steel paring away mercilessly at my old dreams, hopes and attachments. In a flash, gone was the old comfort zone, the illusions about love and la grand passion — all ashes. I entered the adult world. In this world of maturity there is no recourse to blame, but in its place is the ability to see a deeper meaning in everything. In the adult world there are no resentments, no judgements and no disappointments. There is experience, forgiveness, and a radical faith that whatever happens is truly beneficial. In the adult world there is acceptance of others — as we all are — imperfect, afraid, unfinished.

It was from this world that one day I picked up the phone and made three very important phone calls — it was time for me to move on. I spoke to the people from whom I was ruptured and offered my apologies for any pain or upheaval I had been the cause of in New York. What came back to me that morning was a warm torrent of love and forgiveness. Whatever hardness remained of the past melted away, I was free. Feeling uplifted, I realised I had taken an important step towards others, towards myself, and towards God.

Time is a great healer and bringer of perspective. Nothing worth having is won without a struggle as we embrace the spirituality of our imperfection. This God was telling me that I could not undertake my journey alone, I had to do it with others in order to experience conflict and the awareness of my imperfection — without which there is no pain or growth. Only by staying on the path and learning how to walk together, may we attain the perfection of our spirituality.

This rite of passage brought me the gifts of forgiveness, humility and acceptance. As I re-engaged with my spiritual family, the empathy and love flowing my way drew me closer, much closer than before. My initiation was complete.

chapter eighteen

GATHERING LILIES

Our spiritual journey is not one we are meant to make alone. Embracing community is an integral aspect for we spiritual travellers, as together, we move towards communion.

Spiritual community is as successful as the integrity of the philosophy and practice it rests on, and with which it is embraced. No aspect of it will go untested. This seems to be the Law of Spiritual Community. Initiation is a far cry from a glorious ceremonial event, and just as the individual must experience initiation, so must the community as a whole. Rites of passage are as much a part of the development of community as they are of us, individually. The purpose of the spiritual journey is to take us from our lowest point of consciousness to our highest, by reforming our character. In this way the community, too, moves from its lowest point of group consciousness to its highest, as this process of transformation unfolds.

According to legend, in ancient times Mount Parnassus in Greece was sacred to the gods Dionysus and Apollo, and the Muses. With the Castalian spring and Delphi on its slopes, it has come to symbolise the highest human aspirations. It is also home to the native Parnassus Lily, which symbolises the separation of soul and body, and is used as a flower remedy for separation, grief and loss. The task of spiritual community is that we climb the mountain together, as well as alone. The heights of Parnassus await us.

It seems necessary to struggle with all of the issues that arise in community through the levels of both the ego and soul. The learning at the former level is crucial, yet it is in the silence of the soul that psychological and karmic detritus is burned away, finished in the fire of yoga. The real task of the group is partly about the process of each individual becoming whole, but it is also about the process of the group as an entity achieving completion.

People who are making significant spiritual efforts over a long period of time together experience many changes in their relationships, interactions and group dynamics. The coming together of disparate souls through transcendence of the ego forges deep and lasting bonds. Spiritualising of everyone's individual talents, skills, and ability to relate in super-sensuous (beyond the senses) ways, becomes an immense source of inspiration. As the group matures and operates in a unified way, the effect is exceptionally powerful.

For the soul who is undeniably attracted to the higher path one thing is certain, sooner or later it will feel organically appropriate to make a commitment of some kind to that path. This means participating in a spiritual community. Many spiritually motivated people may dislike groups, after all it is much easier to 'do your own thing'. The link between spiritual development and group process is as clear as the line of fate upon your palm. For the soul in isolation, growth is limited because the personality is not activated to such a great extent, whereas interaction with others triggers the ego defences and games of the personality — inciting awareness and growth.

The soul that marches to the beat of a different drum is out of step with mainstream society. When we are called to join together with others who share a common link, we gather for the higher recognition we share, not primarily to make friends or interact socially, that will happen anyway. We come together because we have been called together. Relationships of this nature have a different focus, a different basis. Connecting with a group of people whose recognition is spiritual makes the connection unique.

Once I began to attend various gatherings at the meditation centre, I connected with others who were attending on a regular basis. It occurred to me that in many cases, these were not people I would ever have developed a friendship with under normal circumstances. My lifestyle and circle of friends were rather different. Those of us at meditation were brought together because of a common attraction to the meditation experience and to the knowledge of Raja Yoga. This was a new experience for me. I liked everyone and enjoyed their company. There was an interesting mixture of spiritual depth and agreeable light heartedness in these people, and I found their easy humour reassuring. As I got to know more yogis from further afield, I discovered some very deep and wonderful connections that, over time, have been a source of tremendous growth, companionship and nourishment. I have also had my differences with people along the way, and I would not change any of it! These instances have shown me that what characterises a spiritual relationship is very similar to a successful marriage, the ability to completely let go of differences and move forward in relationship, with tolerance, respect and a forgiving heart.

Working with theatre companies for twenty years taught me much about community. Observing the struggle with group decision making time after time, has often brought echoes of theatrical philosophy shared with me by wise and experienced colleagues reflecting authoritatively on the dynamics of theatre companies. 'Democracy', many have assured me, 'does not work, and decision making by committee does not work'; this is cited as the main reason actors' cooperatives fail. The only system that does work well in theatre is the benevolent monarchy, and it works well because the monarch (the producer or 'management'), selects and engages the actors, director and production team on their individual professional merits, entrusts them to do their job, oversees the administration of the company and is otherwise rather invisible. The boundaries in theatre are very clear and respected, and everyone gets on with their own job unhindered, working towards the same goal, with integration of every area of the production dovetailing before the opening night. Teamwork is the life blood of the performing arts. It is remarkable how a group of professionals can come together on a production, often meeting one another for the first time, and work together in such an inspired way that individuality is completely transcended in deference to the greater task of the group, the production or play. This is communion. It may not occur frequently, but it happens often enough for most seasoned theatre people to have at least several such recollections. An inspiring and visionary director can bring a company of actors and production team into an experience of heightened cooper-ation and exalted creative potential. Spiritual community aims to attain this level of communion in a permanent way, but it can all too easily become derailed when boundaries within the group are transgressed.

Boundaries are one of the most significant issues in the devel-opment of groups and communities. Learning to respect the boundaries of others is a very important part of growing up and is pivotal to spiritual growth. When healthy boundaries are not maintained, or when personalities override the principles of the group, the group can be thrown into chaos.

When people are initially drawn together, the level of group contact is superficial and results in the formation of something that appears to be community, but is not. Pseudo community may abound in sweetness and light. It is a little like taking marriage vows in a pink cloud of romantic intoxication. Rose-coloured glasses and good feelings prevail as people identify with the new-found joy of being together, revelling in the sameness and mutuality that is shared. When the pink cloud disappears, many will disappear with it. Sooner or later difference comes to the fore. True community is akin to a well-tested marriage. Issues of power and difference must be successfully worked through. Differences and resistance exist at the level of ego-personality, but they are not resolved at this level. Words like 'letting-go' and 'forgiveness' speak of the movement of spirit. Bringing a soul-conscious awareness into relationships leads the way through tolerance, acceptance, respect and valuing of difference. True community is forged over a long period of time between souls who get to know one another through changing circumstances, ageing and growth. Power dynamics, games of the status quo and ego are all played out, worked through and ultimately dissolved. It occurs automatically while we are travelling the road together, moving in and out of chaos and integration. True community does not serendipitously 'just happen' between a group of 'nice' people in the course of a weekend. In my experience it takes many years for true community to emerge. Where there is spiritual integrity and a system based on higher values, the possibilities are, at the very least, inspiring.

With reference to the group, I will inevitably experience my fears, jealousy, neediness, desire to control, attachment, dependency, rebellion, avoidance, anger and all of the contents of my own Pandora's box. With spiritual knowledge and power, with awareness and willingness to move beyond the personality, the support is there for me to progress. The movement from old behaviour patterns into awareness is the movement of spirit. Ego-consciousness and duality has been with me since the beginning of recorded history, thus my courage will be tested over and over again in this struggle with the self.

The fire of yoga burns high whenever we gather for this purpose. The capacity to bring about high melting temperatures is greatly enhanced in the group. In India, such an event is called a bhatti, which means sitting in a hot oven or furnace for an extended period. Using the fire of yoga, we can melt down the hard layers of ego that entrap the soul. The little bird will one day realise the cage is unlocked and leave its prison forever, but first it must 'die alive'. Freedom, the gift of courage and determination, is the wings to fly.

The soul within community is balancing and harmonising contradictory drives and impulses for separateness and togetherness, sameness and difference. Respect for difference is intrinsic to community development. Difference is the life-blood of the group. Difference ensures greater resources of creativity, talent, skill, ideas and perspectives. It calls on our ability for patience and tolerance, without which the soul's journey lacks meaning and true community simply cannot evolve. Valuing difference enables us to move beyond the limitations of fear, narcissism and cliqueyness — the obstacles to true community.

Loosely speaking, within a group of this nature there are four streams. First are those who are 'straightlaced', attached to a fundamentalist approach and keen to do it 'by the book', sticking rigidly to a straight and narrow path with which they feel secure. Second are those who are aligned with the philosophy and basic principles but rebel against rigidity and certain trappings of the practice or philosophy. As a result, they like to do a bit of cage rattling. In the third stream are those who are neither rigid nor rebellious, but who integrate spirituality into their lives, relying on their own experience and wisdom to move along their path in a mature, self-supporting and co-operative manner. The fourth stream are completely surrendered and dedicate their whole self, without reservation, in service to God, the community and humankind. They do not have a private or personal life. Most of what they say and do is public. The fourth stream has the fewest numbers, for now at least. True community is incomplete without all four groups.

Beginners in the community may initially identify more strongly with the first stream, then move into the second, and eventually the third. Others may remain fixed in one stream permanently, while some may find themselves identifying with each of the four streams in the course of a day. It is not unusual to feel a shift from one stream to another now and again, but in general terms, there will be a strong identification with one particular stream most of the time. Anyone in these streams may reside either inside the institution or in their own homes, but their choice to do so will be based on very different criteria. As with any model of definition, this is only a very loose frame of reference.

It is quite common for people in one stream to feel subtly threatened by those in another. For example, those with a slightly rigid, fundamentalist approach may encounter their more liberal-minded colleagues with an edge of fear and disdain. Some of the more liberal-minded people may find the 'straightness' of the first stream a little black and white. Cliqueyness develops between people in the same stream of spiritual growth and arises from narcissism and immaturity. Understanding and tolerance of all these streams is imperative in community, because a spiritual community must include, accept and value everyone. When religious or spiritual communities break down, it is often because one of these streams will not tolerate the others. They may even become a polarised faction and decide to break away. Community awareness of these dynamics, and mindfulness of the need to compassionately accommodate the differing needs of these streams, means that all may co-exist in an integrated, harmonious way, with no stream being marginalised or made to feel 'less than' or 'better than' the others. An accomplished leader will be adept at valuing and accommodating the differences. Should an appointed leader emerge from the first or second stream, if they have not worked through their fear of difference, they could either split the group or damage its unity. If all four groups are not represented, the community is not complete. As the community matures and spiritual bonding overrides differ-ences, everyone lets go and the different streams become much more homogeneous. Learning to understand, accept, support, honour and love others equally, regardless of differences or similarities, is the hallmark of spiritual maturity and true community.

A spiritual community is a representation of the family and a microcosm of the larger society. When we first enter a community we experience the dependency or infancy phase of our human development. It is a time when repeated explanation, teaching, nurturing and input is required. This is also a time when we need to be cared for and 'mothered' along. Once our needs at this level have been fully met, we are ready to move into the counter-dependence stage. Characterised by a need to separate and develop our own spiritual identity, this stage involves a power struggle, questioning everything, and deciding what works for us and what does not work. When the needs of this stage have been fully met, we are ready to move into the independence stage. The independent, self-supporting, self-responsible, self-validating person is ready to explore his or her potential and bring it into their life as an expression of their spirituality. They will also have mastered the art of truly caring for and empowering themselves. Finally, the interdependence stage is reached. Cooperation and partnership, caring for and empowering others, serving the community and humankind, are expressions at this level.

Factors which have the capacity to undermine community are splits within the group and leadership styles that are either rigid, controlling, or flaccid. Unless those who are appointed leaders have the attitude of being instruments, of serving a higher purpose rather than themselves and being answerable to a power greater than themselves, their leadership style may be either dictatorial or charismatic, neither of which is aligned with spirituality. Principles must always come before personalities in spiritual community. Leaders must be 'clean', free of attachments to or 'favouring' certain people or 'ways' within the community, and able to unequivocally maintain and protect the integrity of the organisation and its philosophy, at all times. Leading with a balance of strength and sensitivity is vital. The leader who is too strong, rigid or charismatic will acquire followers and invite dependence. Leaders play a vital role in unifying the group, thus the 'divide and conquer' management style has no place in a spiritual environment. The leader who is too sensitive or is primarily concerned with being liked will not be able to maintain clear and healthy group boundaries, make tough decisions or lead. The leader who does not respect and uphold the boundaries and structures of the community, or deal with issues appropriately — especially the difficult ones — as they arise, will betray the community in damaging ways.

'Duty of Care' in a spiritual community must be in the forefront of our awareness. When unethical or unlawful behaviour in a community is covered up, especially by leaders, the consequences are catastrophic. Leaders who avoid taking responsibility, or who compromise group interests, disempower and devalue all group members and abuse the trust that underpins community. Without trust in the leader, community cannot survive. In other words, a leader who does not take responsibility when it is necessary does not lead, and plunges their organisation into chaos. Leaders are often in unenviable positions, but the moment they abandon their ethics and integrity they are doomed — and the community will have to deal with the consequences.

Blocked, stagnant energy can build up in groups when issues are not dealt with appropriately, hence communities really benefit from working at remaining fresh, honest and alive in the face of entropic forces. Creating systems can become a way of trying to avoid blocked energy, and may be a distraction for a community that feels the need to facilitate protection of some kind. It is simply not possible to hold people with systems, you can only draw and hold people with love. Systems are Iron Aged creations. Systems are a replacement for the heart energy that nurtures, forgives, and shifts stagnation. In the future systems will pass into oblivion.

The strongest way to lead is through love. Love generates a more powerful strength of connection than anything else. It is the most powerful motivator and gives strength beyond all others. With love, comes everything.

Of the four streams in community, one group in particular will facilitate the invigorating winds of change. They will emerge from the cobwebs of tradition and attachment to old, fixated ideas, like eagles soaring above a desert. Their role is necessary to shift complacency and outmoded ways that hold the group back. These souls will possess or develop a warrior nature, by necessity, because truth opens the door to change. Naming the truth requires courage and deep discernment. The one who names the truth may be vilified, rejected and feared by those who want to remain stuck. They will also be supported and trusted by those who don't.

In a group that is stuck, I have found that people can be reluctant to identify with two of the four groups. I once asked a group to sort themselves into these streams, and discovered we had lots of threes and fours. One person in the group identified as a two, and another tentatively identified as a one, then moved into the four group. Why was this? Because when a community is stuck there is a lack of risk taking and self-awareness. For some reason, ones and twos are seen to be outside the comfort zone. Of course they exist, but can be hesitant to reveal themselves. This is part of the dynamic of a community that is clinging to phoniness. Everyone wants to look good, but underneath many who identify as threes and fours are chronic, stuck, fence sitters. Many others who are hungry for change get stuck in the system.

A leader who is stuck will cause the energy in the group to stagnate, and this sets up a situation whereby people who are stuck themselves will mostly be attracted to the group. A group with a positive energy flow will attract people who relate to and feel the energy flow, and are pulled by it. Energy is the attractor and has all the answers.

Enlightened 'ones' hold focus for the group, and can be the quiet achievers who deal with much of the basic and practical tasks of the community, while always being mindful and self-aware. They can be a powerful support, and will keep the home fires burning, offering nurture and caring to others.

Without robust, if small, representation in the twos, the group can become stuck and lacking in oxygen. Twos take up the role of questioning and challenging outmoded thinking and the status quo, introducing new ideas, and bringing about change. They keep the energy in the system moving, and seek to free a closed, stagnant system into the open position when it shuts down. They have radar for blocked energy fields, and possess the discernment for what is needed to shake things up.

A visionary leader or manager actively encourages and fosters twos, and may well be a two themselves, but in less enlightened situations the twos may be sidelined. Not that that will stop them. If anything, it fuels their determination. Experience tends to awaken an integrity in twos who sense how to get new ideas filtering into the organisation from the bottom up, when it is clear a full frontal assault will only create massive resistance. Twos learn to be clever and at times subtle in their ways of fostering change, while firmly wed to their purpose. Only as a last resort they will they leave the organisation, more often becoming 'outsiders', finding a way to hold on to the integrity of their spiritual commitment while remaining outside the stagnant, blocked influences.

In the greater society twos can be easy to pick. They are the 'outspoken' souls who name the truth and work relentlessly for change, and whose opinions may be sought by the media on a range of issues. They become a voice within their community, and perhaps on the world stage where their voice can echo through the centuries. From Galileo to Germaine Greer, twos challenge complacency and fuel controversy. Without twos, we'd still be inhabiting a flat earth and rubbing stones together to make fire. Gandhi was one such deeply committed two. An integrated individual, Gandhi would probably have also identified elements of each stream within himself.

Soon after he founded the Satyagraha (meaning force of truth and peace) Ashram in Ahmedabad, an event occurred which challenged Mohandas Gandhi's integrity as a leader. He required the twenty-five members of his ashram to sign a contract when they joined, agreeing to abide by a set of principles that he had drawn up. These included brahmacharya or celibacy, vegetarianism, renunciation of possessions and full acceptance of Untouchables — the casteless lower echelon of Indian society. When a young Untouchable couple and their baby were accepted into the ashram, the ashramites refused to eat their evening meal in protest and complained of being defiled and humiliated. Gandhi's wife, Kasturbai, was so offended she threatened to leave the ashram. Gandhi responded, saying she would have to abide by the rules or leave, adding that they would still be friends. When the cloth merchants who were financing the community threatened to withdraw their financial support over the issue, Gandhi remained unperturbed and said he would move the ashram into the Untouchable section of Ahmedabad, where they would support themselves by doing the manual labouring work of Untouchables. He also adopted the baby of the Untouchable couple, infuriating his wife. Ultimately, financial support was not withdrawn and Gandhi's uncompromising attitude telegraphed a clear message to the community, to India and the world, that the Satyagraha Ashram would not countenance Untouchability![29]

Good leaders, as Gandhi demonstrated time after time, never shrink from responsibility or avoid dealing with the difficult issues facing their community. They put those issues 'on the table' and keep them there until they are resolved. Community cannot grow unless divisive issues are confronted, and real leaders facilitate and support this process.

Being an instrument and leader invariably involves making mistakes and being attacked and derided at times. The strength to learn from these events; to be detached from popularity or alienation, success or failure, attraction or repulsion, poverty or wealth; and to serve the higher purpose of the community regardless, is the hallmark of a truly great soul. True leaders are extremely gifted members of the human race. A great leader is a most loved and loving, gentle, humble, wise, strong and discerning being, who fully lives and embraces the principles and doctrine they are espousing. When asked what makes a good leader during a television interview in Sydney 2002, the Dalai Lama summed it up thus, 'Be truthful, respect the rights of others, be straightforward, build trust — and you can lead.' Fortunately, though it is rare, great leaders do exist.

True community is inclusive, open, and has clearly defined, flexible boundaries. It honours, values and respects the rights of all to be who they are. A true spiritual community accepts and honours the right of anyone to make their own decisions and choices, such as leaving the group without being judged or alienated, and openly accepts and honours those who decide to return.

Within each individual, maturity, self-validation and self-referencing are as important as the ability to recognise and surrender to the greater good of the community, and ultimately of human kind. The power to transcend individuality, to co-operate in the greater task of the group and with other members of the group, is a significant aspect of inner development. Spiritual growth must embrace all of these factors, as well as the deeply personal journey of each individual.

The challenges of being in a group will happen under any circumstance. If stagnation occurs in the affairs of a group, such as when issues are being avoided, the community will swing out of balance and get stuck. Leadership is not just the responsibility of one person, nor is it the job of a leader to 'wipe noses' and listen to petty complaints. In true spiritual community all have a shared responsibility and a contribution to make to the leadership, and there is the space and flexibility for this to occur. The greatest resource in any community is the people themselves, and where enlightened leadership exists all will experience the value and specialness of their own contribution to the group, as well as that of everyone else.

Enlightened leadership encourages and reinforces group autonomy, rather than fostering dependence and infantile behaviour. When leaders have to be consulted over petty decisions and trivial matters, there is a problem around issues of responsibility and maturity within the community.

When a community gets stuck, symptomatic attempts to fix, rescue, control, blame and factionalise the group may follow. Personal agendas may surface. All this is part of the community process. Shake-ups occur whenever the system goes into stagnation, or issues are not being dealt with. Groups must be able to breathe freely; if there is stale air and no oxygen coming in, there is unrest. A group that cannot breathe or continually balance itself will die of asphyxiation or paralysis. Because change is a constant, balancing is also a constant. Nothing stays the same and the wise leader not only understands the cyclic process of community, but intuits and facilitates the vital need for homeostatic balance, movement and growth.

'Dying alive' is a part of this too, it must happen to the group as a whole. M. Scott Peck, in his book *The Different Drum* speculates that 'death' precedes true community.[30] Attempts to control and fix the group eventually give way to surrender. In what he determines to be the final stage of community, silence and peace reign. A new maturity is born, and people are able to listen to one another in a deep and accepting way. It is this death that brings about real bonds rather than superficial ones. Steel is forged by being put in fire, heated until it glows and then beaten.

Afterwards the steel is very much stronger. Spiritual community must go through this process, not once or twice, but again and again.

The ability to ride out uncomfortable times reveals true commitment of community members to the spiritual purpose of the group. A person who is mature, sincere and patient enough to support the group process will reap the benefits. Anyone carrying too much unresolved baggage from their family of origin may well run for cover. Individuals who find they cannot fix, split or control the group may leave, angry and disappointed. Groups are wonderful scenarios for examining personal issues, because these will inevitably be triggered at some point. As the law of karma decrees, with a humble attitude we can recognise our need to hide, avoid, blame, fix or control and let go of that need, rather than let go of the group. The reality is that some will let go of the group and hold blame and bitterness in their hearts.

A spiritual community, like any group, is sure to be rife with projection (the assigning of disowned aspects of the self to another person), and all are susceptible. However, spiritual growth results from moving beyond projections and other ego defences and, as the group matures spiritually, this behaviour lessens. Unresolved family issues may be unconsciously trans-ferred to the group and from this point on, a person uncon-sciously relates to the group as they would to their own family. They cannot see the difference between the group and their own family, and they are oblivious to what they are doing. Coping mechanisms such as gossip and unhealthy alliances severely undermine the community as a whole.

A young man spoke to me repeatedly of how unsupported and undervalued he felt within our community. This occurred over many years, yet my perception was that this fellow was both popular and demonstrably loved, supported and valued more than most people in the community! Eventually he distanced himself, with a long list of complaints about the group. When I learned that his parents had not really 'seen' him, supported or valued him as a child, it became apparent that he was unable to receive the genuine love and valuing of his spiritual family. The bitterness and inherent sense of unworthiness he developed as a child, he now relentlessly blamed the community for. Becoming aware of these dynamics and acknowledging our own past experiences with their link to current reactive patterns, helps us to begin freeing ourselves. The perspective and power that comes with soul-consciousness are invaluable when working through these issues.

Group leaders can attract 'authority figure' projections from group members. When this results in approval-seeking behaviours, rebellion or adoration, it will not foster spiritual growth. Owning our projections, our reactions and unhealthy ways of coping, in order to change, is a vital part of maturing spiritually. When things go wrong, children blame whereas adults take responsibility and focus on how to make the best of a situation. A spiritual community, like any other community, is as good as the strength of character of its individuals. Developing an impeccable and flawless character filled with virtue is the goal of those on the spiritual path, and the task of the community which is truly committed to this goal — to bring about a world of truth and lasting peace.

The coat of arms of India bears the motto: 'Truth Brings Victory.' A time will come when the work is complete, all the lessons learned. The community will be as one, in harmony with one thought, one mind, one consciousness, one voice, one heart and one love. As one, we will ultimately 'die alive', and all external affiliation, group identity, and structure, will be totally incinerated.

Then together, on the heights of Parnassus, we will gather lilies — the symbol of victory — and the soul will be set free.

chapter nineteen

DANCE *of* LIFE

There are many paths we may take in this life. Some lead to higher ground, others into the seductive underworld of illusion, but all lead to experience and knowledge. Whichever road the spiritual traveller chooses is valid. In Herman Hesse's tale, Siddhartha's journey could not be complete until he had explored and experienced the path of the senses in order to come full circle.[31] Spirituality is about wholeness of being through conscious awareness and choice. Choosing the path of realisation is to be and to express the true self rather than the false ego-personality.

After experiencing the loss of his spirituality through years of immersion in lust, greed and sensual indulgence, Siddhartha returns to the river where he fasts from his senses, listens to the river and is mentored by the solitary ferryman who offers him respite. There, Siddhartha's greatest challenge is played out, when he is rejected by his beloved son to Kamala. Siddhartha is forced to face the excruciating suffering of attachment and settle the karmic account he created when leaving his own father, never to return. Freeing himself of this attachment is his final, most shattering crisis.

The knowledge and learning that is attained by walking the spiritual path is essentially the story of defeat and victory of the self over the self. There is no external enemy, no physical battle, no *jihad* or 'holy war'. The prize of victory is freedom from the prison of the senses and ego, leading to inner peace and enlightenment. To know the self means knowing the full light of the soul and the extreme darkness of the personality. The soul's journey may take place over many lifetimes, as we travel through time knowing the heights of love, joy and freedom; and the pain of defeat, loss and separation. The 'old soul' has lived many lives, followed many spiritual and religious paths in their search for meaning, and gained much experience in the game of life. For this reason the old soul will thirst for truth and spiritual wisdom. The flame of yearning, however, will not be satisfied with simplistic, hollow answers or practices that lack integrity.

It is at this time, the Diamond Age, the brief and most powerful time of the cycle between the Iron Age and the Golden Age, that the soul completes its journey. The pull to one path or another is a hallmark of this time in history, as each of us finds our spiritual place of belonging in the larger scheme of things. It may involve finding an inner, personal connection with God or it may be with Christ, Buddha, Abraham, Mohammed, with a yogi or guru, or none of these. The prophet souls have provided a way of understanding through their teachings, and a way of being through the example of their life. The important recognition is that we are a very large spiritual family, characterised by our uniqueness and diversity, our mutuality and empathy. In our difference, we have so much richness to exchange and share; in our similarities lie essential connection and comfort. For a moment, in the Diamond Age, we may observe the variety and beauty of the great human family tree as it reaches its fullness. The Being of Light shines upon the whole tree of souls, with all of its branches of religions and spiritual traditions, and upon all souls no matter who or where we are, regardless of whether we pray, meditate, chant or just have our own private thoughts.

Buddha, Mohandas Gandhi, Christ, Abraham, Mohammed, Guru Nanak (founder of the Sikh religion), the Dalai Lama, Socrates, Confucius, Lao Tse, Aristotle, Plato, St Augustine, Hildegard of Bingen, St Francis of Assisi, Clare of Assisi and Mother Theresa, together with many other well-known and less well-known souls who populate the religions, philosophies and spiritual paths, have revealed a common dedication to their pursuit of truth and wholeness. Practices and philosophies may differ, but when we embrace our chosen path in a wholehearted, balanced and loving way, we integrate it into our daily life and way of being. To follow truly does not mean to follow out of fear, or with rigidity or force, for the way of the heart is the way of ease, surrender, courage and maturity. It means inevitable discomfort at times because truth cannot be compromised. There is no possibility of compromise if we wish to develop spiritually. Self-sovereignty is the prize of total surrender to the Being of Light. Herein lies the challenge of spiritual endeavour. Those who embark upon this journey will never know boredom, as the inner life bursts into blossom and begins to thrive. The call of destiny and spiritual love is an irresistible force that cannot be ignored.

ৡৣ৹৵ঌ

In the late 1970s I was tentatively invited to go to America and do some work there. I had never wanted to go to the USA, but for some reason the prospect pulled me, and as my life had reached a junction a complete change was also attractive. Before I left, an acquaintance who was an astrologer summoned me to tell me what my chart revealed about all this. I listened in disbelief as he implored me not to go, because, he claimed, very heavy karmic accounts awaited me in America. It was his belief that living in America would 'break me'. He urged me to remain in Australia, where, he declared, my karma was very positive, adding that I had some strange patterns in my chart which revealed I had the chart of a nun. 'Your mother must have your birth time wrong', he said. I agreed. Nonetheless, he continued, 'During your life a great spiritual awakening will occur and the consciousness of humanity will shift from extreme materialism to spirituality, just like turning an hourglass upside-down. It will happen suddenly and it will originate in the East. You will be part of this change of consciousness,' he said. 'You — your life will change dramatically, the world as we know it will disappear and a new age will come.'

Not even the remotest, smallest part of me could relate to any of this, in fact I thought he was quite mad. 'Please don't go to America!' were his final words as I left. He hugged me and then placed a cassette in my hand, I could hardly believe he had even put all that on tape. As I walked down the street I shrugged all of it off as complete nonsense and seeing an open garbage bin, threw the tape into it and headed for the car. To say it had gone straight over my head was an understatement. I did not give anything he said another thought. Shortly after this meeting I heard he had disappeared and wondered about his mental health. Within two weeks I was on a flight bound for America, despite the fact that the person who had invited me in the first place had changed their mind and did not go.

Within five years the astrologer's warnings and predictions were ringing in my ears. How I wished I had not thrown the tape away. He had missed one vital part of the plot, though. America was where my destiny lay. The force which drew me to my destiny would not be put off, and had I been more aware at the time and listened to him, it is possible I would not have gone. The unseen forces which really shape our lives are usually not at all foreseeable or recognisable, yet we get drawn into step, we dance with them. This is the unknowable, mystical, magical dance of life; a dance that never ends, testing our agility and flexibility as it leads us through unpredictable twists and turns. When we become complacent we fall, our wisdom and experience vanish.

By the late 1980s I had spent almost ten years in the USA, and about twenty years away from Australia. In the space of a weekend the call of destiny sounded unmistakably, yet again. Two vital factors in my life changed very suddenly after a Raja

Yoga retreat in San Francisco. After catching up with friends until very late on Sunday evening, I flew back to LA on the milk run, arriving home about 2 am. A telephone message greeted me, informing me that the house I had lived in all the time I had been in LA had been sold. The next morning I went to work, discovering immediately that everyone in the studio had finally been laid off due to an extremely protracted writers' strike. I felt a lightness open up inside me which rapidly turned into joy. My karma in America was over at last, without notice. Straight away, I went to buy a ticket to Australia, and within hours I began to feel like a caged animal desperate for release. Three weeks later I flew home to Sydney.

Amid all the farewells, the familiar and warm connections I was letting go, I had the overriding sense that my life had reached a fullness or completion on the one hand, and an emptiness on the other. Nostalgia gripped me as I said goodbye to the people with whom I shared the bond of awakening. Witnessing spiritual birth and growth in one another with all the attendant intoxication, camaraderie and sometimes drama this evokes is a unique experience. Others would never know us in quite the same way we knew one another. As I began expressing these sentiments a quiet, unassuming Indian fellow commented affectionately, 'Judi sister, when you came on the scene I thought God had gone completely mad. I thought, he's crazy if he thinks he can change her. Now, I have so much faith!'

The person who returned to Australia was not quite the person who left. A little less cynical, a theist now, in a deeply personal relationship with God, following a brahmacharya lifestyle, and connected with a spiritual movement from the East. How strange this seemed, and what a very odd thing to be doing, I thought, wondering how on earth I was going to explain myself to all my old friends 'downunder'. Would they accept me the way my friends in America had, I wondered? I thought about the astrologer too. From my 'awakened' perspective, he was, of course, not mad, he was a visionary. No doubt it was very difficult for him to say those things to me before I left.

I have learned that what is often the difference between labelling an idea crazy or brilliant, is time. In the web of materialism and the blindness of ego it may be difficult to envision a spiritual revolution, a change in world consciousness occurring so rapidly, that it will be like turning an hourglass upside down. Yet silently, irretrievably, the sand is running out.

Glossary

ahimsa   ancient Jain commandment meaning non-violence to all living things

Being of Light   Supreme Soul

bhatti   to sit in yoga for an extended period of time in order to create an intense spiritual heat or fire of yoga; literal meaning: oven

brahmacharya   purity

Brahma Kumaris (BK)   the organisation founded in 1937 in India, dedicated to the task of creating world peace through inner peace and human spiritual upliftment. The Brahma Kumaris is administered by women, and has consultative status on the Economic and Social Council of the United Nations and UNICEF. The organisation offers courses in Raja Yoga meditation free of charge, and runs a variety of educational programs and retreats for people from all walks of life, internationally. The BKs welcome people from all faiths and spiritual paths.

'dying alive'   ego death; the act of sacrificing a part of the ego in service of spiritual growth

ego-personality   as distinct from the spiritual personality, refers to the adapted or false self, ego defences, coping mechanisms, roles

eight powers   Power to Discern, Power to Judge, Power to Pack Up, Power to Accommodate, Power to Tolerate, Power to Withdraw, Power to Face, Power to Co-operate

false ego   as above, a phoney or inauthentic construction of self

Higher Being   Supreme Soul

law of karma   law of action, or of cause and effect

natural laws   laws of karma

Raja Yoga meditation   open-eyed meditation that facilitates a connection with the soul or true self, and the Supreme Soul *realisations* flashes of insight or sudden understanding

sadhana spiritual effort

samana a renunciate who seeks to be completely free from ego

satsang a spiritual gathering; literal meaning: in the company of truth

satyagraha a term coined by Mohandas Gandhi meaning force of truth, love and peace

self-contemplation awareness focused on 'I' the soul

self-knowledge knowledge of the spiritual or true self

Supreme Soul the Source, Creator or God

soul-consciousness a state of altered or higher consciousness (as opposed to the consciousness of the ego), achieved through meditation

spiritual allergies conscious or unconscious feelings of betrayal, disappointment, fear, resistance, hurt, anger or bitterness towards a parent, caregiver or religious representative, which is unconsciously transferred onto a Higher Power or God, causing a rupture in the relationship with a Higher Power

spiritual 'organs' or faculties the subtle faculties; mind, intellect, conscience, will, memory, awareness, heart

subtle self soul, true self or spirit

super sensuous experiences an experience beyond the physical senses (for example, super-sensuous joy)

synchronicity a juxtaposition of unusual events or coincidences which are linked and may represent a symbolic meaning or sign

true self soul, spirit or subtle self

yoga connection or link between the soul and Supreme Soul; also means yoke or union

Endnotes

1   William Shakespeare, *Julius Caesar*, Activ. Sc.iii. L.217, Oxford University Press, Oxford, 1905.

2   Raymond A. Moody Jr, *Life After Life*, Bantam Books, New York, 1976.

3   Herman Hesse, *Siddhartha*, 1922, translation Joachim Neugroschel, Penguin Books, England, 1999.

4   Heinrich Harrer, *Seven Years in Tibet*, JP Tarcher Inc., Los Angeles, 1953.

5   Shirley MacLaine, *Out on a Limb*, Bantam Books, New York, 1983.

6   *Ibid.*, back cover.

7   Sudhir Kakar, *The Analyst and the Mystic*, Viking, Penguin Books, India, 1991, p.x.

8   Raymond A. Moody Jr, *op. cit.*, pp.58–59.

9   Frederick Perls, 'Four Lectures' in *Gestalt Therapy Now*, Joen Fagan and Irma Lee Shepherd, eds, Penguin Books, England, 1972, p.30.

10 Oscar Wilde, *The Picture of Dorian Grey*, *Lippincott's Magazine*, England, 1890.

11 Galatians 6:7.

12 Judith Pemell, *Recovery — An Inner Awakening*, Alcohol and Drug Foundation, Queensland, 1993.

13 Alexandre Dumas, *My Memoirs*, Chilton Company, Philadelphia, 1961.

14 Alcoholics Anonymous, *Big Book*, Step 3.

15 Elizabeth Kübler-Ross, *On Death and Dying*, Tavistock Publications, London, 1969.

16 Jeremy Rifkin, *Entropy*, Viking Press, New York, 1980.

17 Pardon E. Tillinghast, *Approaches to History*, Prentice-Hall, Englewood Cliffs, NJ, 1963, p.9.

18 *Ibid.*, p.11.

19 Yogesh Chadha, *Rediscovering Gandhi*, Century Books, London, 1997.

20 *Living Values: An Educational Program*, <www.livingvalues.net>

21 Diane Tillman, *Living Values Activities for Children Ages 8–14*. Deerfield, FL: HCI, 2000.

22 Diane Tillman, 'Educating for a Culture of Peace in Refugee Camps' in *Childhood Education Magazine, International Focus Issue* 2001, 77(6), pp.375–378.

23 Herman Hesse, *op. cit.*

24 Judith Lewis Herman, *Trauma and Recovery*, Basic Books, Pandora Edition, USA, 2001.

25 Yogesh Chadha, *op. cit.*, p.247.

26 *Ibid.*

27 *Ibid.*, p.460.

28 *Ibid.*

29 *Ibid.*

30 M. Scott Peck, *The Different Drum*, Rider & Co., Great Britain, 1989.

31 Herman Hesse, *op. cit.* 227

Judith Pemell is a Sydney-based counsellor and educator in inner development, with a professional background that includes treating addictions. Her work in the field has been presented to the World Health Organisation in Geneva by special invitation. She became a practitioner of Raja Yoga meditation in 1984 and has spent much time in India studying Eastern spirituality. She travels internationally to conduct seminars and workshops.

B O O K S

O is a symbol of the world, of oneness and unity. In different cultures it also means the "eye," symbolizing knowledge and insight. We aim to publish books that are accessible, constructive and that challenge accepted opinion, both that of academia and the "moral majority."

Our books are available in all good English language bookstores worldwide. If you don't see the book on the shelves ask the bookstore to order it for you, quoting the ISBN number and title. Alternatively you can order online (all major online retail sites carry our titles) or contact the distributor in the relevant country, listed on the copyright page.

See our website www.o-books.net for a full list of over 500 titles, growing by 100 a year.

And tune in to myspiritradio.com for our book review radio show, hosted by June-Elleni Laine, where you can listen to the authors discussing their books.

MySpiritRadio